Successful Table Tennis

Letts**Guide**

Successful
Table Tennis

Peter Simpson

WORLD OF SPORT

World of Sport is produced by
LWT for the ITV network.
This series is published in collaboration
with World of Sport by
Charles Letts & Co Ltd
London Edinburgh München & New York

First published 1980
by Charles Letts & Co Ltd
Diary House, Borough Road, London SE1 1DW

Technical Editor: John Crooke
House Editor: Liz Davies
Design: Perera
Colour photographs: All-Sport Photographic Ltd
Illustrations: Sports Art Ltd
Black and white photographs: All-Sport Photographic Ltd, Mark Moylan
except pp 18, 68, 74, 77 by J. and C. Taylor of Millom, p6 Földy (Switzerland)

Cover shows Milan Orlowski
Frontispiece shows Stellan Bengtsson

The author would like to thank his wife Pat for her help in
preparing the manuscript and players Kenny Jackson and
Dougie Johnson for modelling for the black and white photographs

ISBN: 0 85097 4828

Printed and bound by Charles Letts (Scotland) Ltd

Contents

Introduction

When people ask me what I do for a living, and I tell them I coach table tennis, more often than not the response is, 'Oh, I play table tennis'. What they really mean is that they have knocked a poor little cellulose ball about either on holiday, at home in the garage, at work, at a youth or sports club, and have enjoyed it.

Table tennis is played in all walks of life and appeals to all age groups. There are competitions for those under eleven years of age to veterans of over forty. In fact, table tennis can, and does, span a lifetime of enjoyment. You can find competitions to suit all abilities whether you play at school, college, work, youth club, in a holiday competition, or in an organised tournament – such is the span of table tennis.

Many people start playing table tennis just for fun but, as they improve, their interest snowballs and they become fanatics of a fascinating sport. My intention in this book is to give the aspiring player an insight into the various styles of play. There are many books about table tennis for the beginner covering only the basic strokes. In this book, although I will remind you of these basic principles, I will be moving on to intermediate and advanced stages of play.

In recent years, table tennis has undergone rapid development throughout the world. One of the reasons for this is the introduction of new materials which allows for many combinations, giving a wide variety of racquet types. The sport has not been slow to introduce new techniques to accommodate the new-found technology. Because of this, the sport has reached new boundaries and the variations in styles of play, together with a greater variety of strokes, make the game more flexible. Players today are imparting greater speed, spin and power to their strokes, thus making the sport more dynamic. There has emerged from this a number of original styles of play, developed by particular countries, such as the dynamic topspin of the Hungarians, the drive style of Sweden, but none more original than the variety of styles that has come from China. They have close-to-the-table drive players, or allround players, who are equally effective with their backspin or drive technique. In addition the players have an invincible repertoire of services which they disguise so well. The techniques the Chinese have introduced have made them table tennis masters of the world.

The author giving some advice to Desmond Douglas

Chapter 1 **Making ready**

Racquets

The selection of a racquet needs careful consideration as there are a number of important factors to take into account. Basically, there are three different types of racquet (Fig. 1):

Defensive (slow)
Allround (medium)
Offensive (fast)

But, each racquet has many variations and combinations. There are three different factors to be considered in the make-up of your racquet:

1 The type of wood
2 The type of sponge
3 The type of rubber

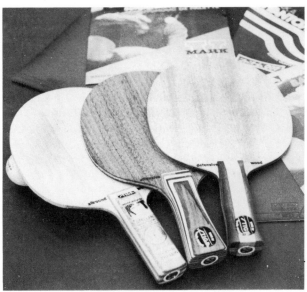

Fig. 1 A selection of blades and rubbers

Type of wood

The blade of a racquet can be made from 1-, 3-, 5- or 7-plywood, but the 5-ply blade is the one most commonly used. Usually, there are three types of wood which can be used in varying combinations to give different effects when playing strokes (Fig. 2).

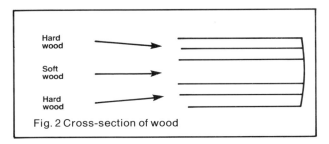

Fig. 2 Cross-section of wood

Defensive blade

This is mainly used by backspin players who like to control the ball and to slow the ball up when strokes are being played. The reason for this is that the middle ply usually contains a layer of soft wood, which slows the ball down as it leaves the racquet.

Allround blade

This is used by players who use control strokes in their play. This type of blade will give good spin and is also good for hitting, therefore it is suitable for both drive and topspin players.

Offensive blade

This is made from a hard type of wood which makes the ball leave the racquet quickly, giving an excessive amount of spin or speed from the stroke. But a word of warning – you will need good control to use this type of blade and many players sacrifice control of the ball by using this blade early on in a rally, for example, when receiving a service. If your opponent has good spin services and you cannot control them because of the type of blade and rubber you are using, then you are wasting your time playing. Do not sacrifice control for the extra spin or speed. Let it be *you* who produces the spin and speed; do not leave it all to the racquet. The next consideration is to marry a suitable sponge and rubber to the blade.

Type of sponge

The sponge is attached to the rubber. The thickness of the sponge is an influencing factor over the amount of control, spin and speed that can be applied to a stroke. The sponge comes in varying thicknesses: 1.0mm; 1.5mm; 2.0mm; 2.5mm. The properties and thickness of the sponge have an effect on the rubber. If the sponge is soft and is on a defensive blade, this will make the racquet slow. If the sponge is hard and on an offensive blade, this will tend to make the racquet fast and also produce excessive spin, which could be difficult for some players to control.

Type of rubber

Again, there are many different types of rubber that could be attached to the sponge, with the pimples either in or out. Each would have a different effect upon the ball. There are varying lengths of pimples, which are approximately between 1.0mm and 2.5mm; they also vary in thickness.

Pimples in

The playing surface is smooth with the pimples on the inside. This playing surface is the most commonly used in today's game. With this type of surface the player can produce maximum spin and speed as there is no restriction on the smooth surface.

Pimples out

This type of playing surface, with the pimples out, gives a lesser degree of topspin, but gives the player good control, and also tends to keep the ball low.

There is a racquet to suit all types of player and all styles of play. Many retailers today sell just the blade, so that you can select the type of rubber you want to use. It could be a combi-racquet – pimples in on one side and pimples out on the other. You will see how this type of racquet can be used, in Chapter 8 on page 65. So, the selection of a racquet needs great consideration. You should ensure that you can control the returns from various styles of opponent, and also see that you can execute the shots for your own particular style of play.

Care of the racquet

It is important to keep the playing surface clean on a pimples in racquet, as this collects dirt and grease from the ball. These properties affect the racquet, causing loss of control, and you will find that you cannot impart spin as the ball will skid off the rubber. It is therefore advantageous to keep the surface clean by gently wiping the rubber with a damp cloth, making sure that it is thoroughly dried afterwards.

Grip

There are two basic styles of grip: the shakehand and the penhold. There are, however, many variations to these grips so you must consider carefully and choose a grip which will suit you and your style of game. A player with away-from-the-table backspin style would be ill-advised to adopt a penhold grip, as this is better for a drive style. When selecting a grip, see that you can play both backhand and forehand strokes without changing your grip too much, and that the backhand is not neglected because the grip you use favours heavy spin with your forehand. Let us look at some of the grips that can be used.

Shakehand shallow grip

The forefinger is extended along the bottom of the blade. The thumb is relaxed on the blade. This type of grip will give you both control and power and it is favoured by the topspin or drive style player. The relaxed grip gives much more freedom, allowing fast movements that are essential when spinning or hitting the ball. The shallow grip also covers a weak point of many shakehand players, and that is the ability to create the correct racquet angle against any type of return, in particular, a ball that is played just over the net (Figs. 3A and 3B). This is achieved by the player being able to make correct use of the wrist when playing strokes.

Shakehand deep grip

This grip is favoured by the backspin player. The player has firm control over the racquet, as he will in the main, be receiving fast, or spinning returns away from the table. The movements of the backspin player when playing his strokes are not as fast as his topspin or drive counterparts, thus giving good backspin

9

Fig. 3A Shakehand shallow grip, forehand

Fig. 3B Shakehand shallow grip, backhand

Fig. 4A Shakehand deep grip, forehand

Fig. 4B Shakehand deep grip, backhand

Desmond Douglas shows the agility needed in table tennis

Fig. 5A Penhold – Japanese style forehand

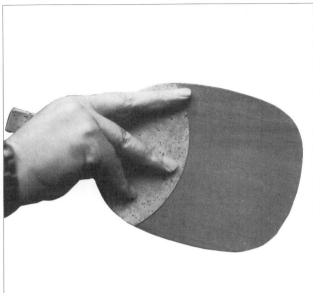

Fig. 5B Penhold – Japanese style backhand

Fig. 6A Penhold – Chinese style forehand

Fig. 6B Penhold – Chinese style backhand

strokes. With this type of grip, it may be difficult to attack a short return over the table (Figs. 4A and 4B).

Penhold - *Japanese style*

With this grip the thumb is deeply inserted at the lower part of the blade and the fingers are extended straight. This grip favours forehand topspin or drive. The fingers on the back of the racquet will give greater power, but this makes backhand strokes difficult to execute, and it can be especially difficult to obtain the correct angle of the racquet (Figs. 5A and 5B).

Penhold - *Chinese style*

Again, the grip is rather deep around the lower part of the blade at the handle, with the thumb the same as for the Japanese style, but with the fingers bunched on the back of the racquet. This style gives better control and movement on both backhand and forehand as the wrist can be incorporated in the stroke, enabling the player to apply varying degrees of angle. This grip is favoured by the Chinese hitters and blockers (Figs. 6A and 6B).

Remember that adopting a particular grip to suit your strong points may leave your weak side exposed.

Adopt a grip so that the racquet is an extension of the playing arm. It is advisable, if you are going to be a topspin or a drive player, that the racquet should be slightly heavier than that used by a backspin player. A racquet that is heavy will give you more spin or speed when playing your strokes. Likewise, if you are a backspin player, a lighter racquet could be advantageous to absorb spin and speed from your opponent's return, but if you want to be adventurous, you could go for a heavy racquet. With this you would lose a certain amount of control, but if you are dextrous enough, you will be able to impart a great deal more spin and you will be able to hit harder.

The penhold player's racquet is usually much lighter than the shakehand racquet. The blade of the racquet on a shakehand style has two sheets of rubber whereas a penhold racquet usually has only one. If you had two racquets, one light and one heavy, and you played a shot with each at identical speed, the heavier racquet would impart more spin and possibly more speed to the ball than the light one. The heavier racquet is capable of imparting a greater degree of spin to the ball, and it will also produce a faster hit. But, before you race off to buy a heavy racquet, be advised that your arms should be relatively strong as you have to swing at great speed. An element of speed and endurance is needed in the arm and, if this has to be executed close to the table, it could be difficult for you to recover into a basic ready position.

There are various ranges of rubbers and racquets in both style and weight for both penhold and shakehand players, and these are necessary as no one racquet will be ideal for everyone. The choice of racquet is determined by the individual techniques and abilities of the player. Therefore, it becomes vital when choosing a racquet and selecting a grip that both should suit your skills, technique and style of play. You may find great satisfaction in using the penhold grip of the Chinese or Japanese, or in using the shallow shakehand grip, or you may favour the deep grip of the shakehand, which is good for backspin players. The ball is in your court – make your choices carefully.

Developing technique

A successful player is one who has a sound basic technique when playing his strokes, and one who can execute a skilled action with precision. He can also perform these skills under the many varying conditions met during training and competition.

Good technique is related to the ability to develop the required level of co-ordination to perform a specific movement. To be able consistently to perform good technique, it is important for you to spend a great deal of time practising and grooving these specific movements so that they become ingrained. A player therefore needs to spend a great deal of time building up a series of movement patterns so that they become habitual. The conditioning of these movement patterns is one of the most important factors in skill learning and is vital especially when introducing the

13

skills and technique into a competitive situation. By building a series of these conditioned movement patterns, a player should acquire well-timed muscular co-ordination. When developing a certain technique you should try to relate it to the conditions that you will meet in a competitive situation. For example, the type of return received will be constantly changing from a ball with very little spin, to one with excessive spin; a slow floating ball, to a ball coming at speed. These various returns will also be delivered from various angles of the table. With this in mind, the type of stroke used should be specific to the ball received. This applies not only to the movement pattern involved but also to the speed of movement, the force exerted and the amount of taction (touch) required.

The interaction between the correct movement, speed, force and taction is necessary to obtain optimal results in the playing of a stroke. You should not think of playing one type of stroke such as a forehand backspin, backhand block, or forehand topspin; to enable you to execute a forehand backspin, practising and playing just one type of forehand backspin stroke will be of no use – you need to be able to play at least three varied strokes and these will be built up as a particular movement pattern for that stroke. Let us look at a stroke and see what is required to play it successfully.

These basic factors govern the successful stroke:

1　**Stroke**
　　This can be played either forehand or backhand.
2　**Form**
　　This is the length of a stroke and is governed mainly by the stance. The form can be *short*, *medium* or *long*.
3　**Stance**
　　This is the base of a player. Good stance means good balance which is needed to take the full movement of the stroke. It can be *square*, *side*, *side-square*.
4　**Speed of ball**
　　Slow, medium, fast.

5　**Spin**
　　Float, topspin, backspin, sidespin. (See section on spin.)
　　When thinking of spin, a floating ball in table tennis terms is a ball with minimum spin. Pure sidespin is rarely used; it is usually a combination of topspin and sidespin or backspin and sidespin which is imparted to the ball, making it spin on an angled axis. (See also Chapter 2 on Spin.)
6　**Timing**
　　Timing is related to the contact point of racquet and ball – these are early, peak of bounce, late (Fig. 7).

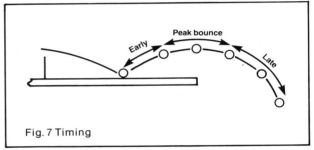

Fig. 7 Timing

7　***Position in relationship to the table***
　　This is the position that you move into to play your stroke. Over the table, end of table, away from the table.

Fig. 8 Basic factors in stroke play

Stroke	Form	Stance	Speed of ball	Spin on ball	Timing	Table position
Forehand	Short	Square	Slow	Float	Early	Over table
Backhand	Medium	Side	Medium	Topspin	Peak of bounce	End of table
	Long	Side-square	Fast	Back-spin	Late	Away from table
				Sidespin		

Good use of the free arm by Guo Yuehua

As you will see, there are many varying positions, timings, number of strokes and also combinations of spin and speed that can be applied to the ball. So, when playing a stroke you must be organised into position to play your strokes by using the various movement patterns (see also Fig. 8).

Ready stance

Table tennis is a sport in which there is a variety of strokes and successive movements, where the ball has various spins, travels different courses at various speeds over relatively short distances and periods of time. To play an effective stroke you need a good basic ready stance to be prepared for any return, especially when a rally is being played at a fast pace. This means that you not only have to control or attack the spin and possibly also the speed of the ball received, but you must also control your own body balance and movements. Being well balanced so that you can achieve good movement is very important. It is this that differentiates table tennis from many other sports which start with the preparation and end with a follow-through. The ready stance is the stance which a player will take up first of all when receiving service and subsequently after playing each stroke in a rally.

The following elements make up the basic ready position:

1 The feet are placed slightly wider than the shoulders
2 The knees are relatively close together, placing the weight on the inside of the feet
3 The player keeps a relatively low stance with the waist and knees bent, so that quick movement in any direction is possible
4 The elbows form a 90 degree angle and are not too close to the body. This again is for quick movement of the arms
5 The player is relaxed and ready to take the necessary action

This low stance assists quick movement and, except for very young or small players, allows you

Fig. 9A Ready stance, sideview

to perceive the ball far more effectively than you would if you had an erect stance (Figs. 9A and 9B).

Because many of the strokes used today are played with a forward motion, it is important to take up a position at least one metre away from the table. This will enable you to move forward into the field of play. After playing the stroke you should then return to the one metre distance, into a ready stance, covering the

Fig. 9B Ready stance, frontview

Fig. 9C Ready stance for a drive or topspin player

particular line of play. If you stand too close to the table to receive service or to play your strokes, you will only be able to use an arm action in the stroke, thus being able to make only a weak return.

The ready stance varies with the style of play:

1   *Drive or topspin*
    The stance is usually taken up on the backhand side of the table as the player of these styles favours using his forehand strokes, which are usually the strongest. The feet positioning will vary, depending upon where the opponent is serving from. If your opponent is serving from the backhand side of the table the feet will be positioned as shown in Fig. 9C, but if he is serving from the forehand side of the table, the feet should be adjusted to be square to your opponent. It is important to adjust your stance in relation to where your opponent is serving from.

17

Fig. 10 Jonyer (Hungary) receiving service

Fig. 11 Jonyer receiving from the opposite corner

Fig. 10 shows Jonyer (Hungary) receiving service. Note that his ready position is square to the server and that his right foot is directed towards his forehand side in anticipation of a service wide to the forehand. In Fig. 11 Jonyer is receiving from the opposite corner. Again he is square to the server but this time to the right of the table.

2 *Backspin*

The backspin player could take up the ready stance approximately at the centre position at the table, and again about one metre away from the table. A backspin player needs to be strong on both wings, that is, on both forehand and backhand (Fig. 12).

18

Fig. 12 Ready stance for a backspin player

Stance when playing a stroke

We have just talked about the ready stance, and we will now look at the stance that is required when playing a particular stroke. This differs from stroke to stroke and is one of the reasons why, after a stroke is played, you should resume a ready stance from which you can take up the playing stance for a specific stroke.

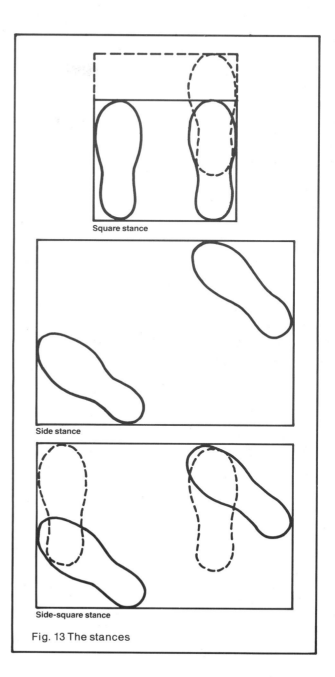

Square stance

Side stance

Side-square stance

Fig. 13 The stances

The stance is known as the base of a player: this is the area that the feet cover while the player is executing his strokes. There are three different types of stance for players to adopt (Fig. 13):

1 Square stance
2 Side stance
3 Side-square stance

(When we talk about stance, this is to the line of play and not to the table.)

Square stance

The square stance is mainly used for control play at the end of the table. With this type of stance it is difficult to put a great deal of power into a stroke as the area that the feet take up (the base) is relatively small.

Side stance

This stance is used for power strokes or when a player is away from the table to allow him plenty of time to recover into a ready position.

Side-square stance

When using this stance the change is performed in one movement. Again it is used mainly in power strokes where a dynamic stroke is executed in a side stance position and there is a follow-through co-ordinating feet and body, going into the ready position.

Form for basic strokes

Form is a combination of many of the basic principles required when playing strokes. The basic principles involved are *playing stance, preparation* and *weight transference*. Strokes are made up of many movement patterns involving the varied movements that are required to meet the strength and complexity of each stroke. To play a stroke with good form you need to be in control of your movements and also to maintain balance throughout the stroke. The emphasis in today's game is *power*, whether you are driving or spinning the ball, thus the basic principle and technique of many of the strokes played today is playing with a forward motion. The first of the basic principles to take into consideration is that of the

stance required when playing the stroke. Without a good stance the playing of the stroke could be difficult to execute. As I have said before, the stance is the base of a player and should at all times be able to take the movement of the stroke, which is basically the length of the stroke, be it short, medium or long (Figs. 14A, 14B and 14C).

The second basic principle is the *preparation* of the stroke. Some coaches maintain that there are three phases to a stroke; they are *preparation, contact*

Fig. 14A Short form

and *follow-through*. I would like to suggest to you that there are only two and these are *preparation* and *contact*. All strokes start with a preparatory movement; this is a fundamental part of the stroke. Once you have made contact with the ball there is nothing you can do to adjust or alter the spin, speed or direction of the ball. Furthermore, most of the strokes today are so ballistic in nature that once they are initiated there is no way of stopping or adjusting the

movement. If you watch the movement of top players, you will see that there is one continuous flowing movement from the ready position preparation, to contact, to ready position. It is not a stop, start, stop sequence.

The third basic principle is that of *weight transference*. When preparing for a stroke, you need to be able to transfer your weight. In this way you will gain maximum effect when playing your stroke, and

Fig. 14B Medium form

Fig. 14C Long form

thus achieve *good form*. None of your power will be wasted if you move into a good position to play the stroke and if you maintain stability so that your weight can be transferred in a specific direction. One of the key factors in weight transference is that the foot taking the weight should be pointing in the direction where the weight is being transferred. However, there may be times when it is impossible to move into a good stable position so, adjust your position by using only the upper part of the body by rotating from the trunk to achieve weight transference.

Playing arm

There are three basic arm positions that can be used (Fig. 15):
1   Half arm
2   Three-quarter arm
3   Full arm
The angle for the half arm is around 90 degrees at the elbow and is mainly used for control play. The three-quarter arm is around 120 degrees and the full arm around 180 degrees at the elbow. The two latter arm angles can be used for the more powerful strokes such as the powerful forehands.

The type of stroke being played and the position in relationship to the table will determine, to a great extent, the angle of the playing arm. For example, if you are close to the table it would be advantageous to use a half arm angle so that you can recover quickly into a ready position. If you use a three-quarter arm or full arm close to the table, you should ensure that you can recover and return to the ready position quickly. When playing with the three-quarter or full arm angle, it is more advantageous to play away from the table, as this will give you more organisational time.

When playing a stroke, a single or a combination of joints in the playing arm can be used:
1   Wrist
2   Elbow
3   Shoulder

Power

In the playing arm there are slow moving parts and fast moving parts. The wrist has the quickest movement and the shoulder has the slowest. These factors need to be taken into consideration if the element of speed is introduced into a stroke. If, however, we are looking for power from the playing arm, the shoulder is where it can best be generated, but very little power can be achieved from the wrist. If you are receiving service, you may use your wrist and elbow; if pushing the ball with the backhand, you may only use the elbow; on a powerful forehand loop you could combine wrist, elbow and shoulder. As you can see, when playing a stroke the effect and efficiency of the combination and co-ordination of the varying sections in the playing arm need to be considered.

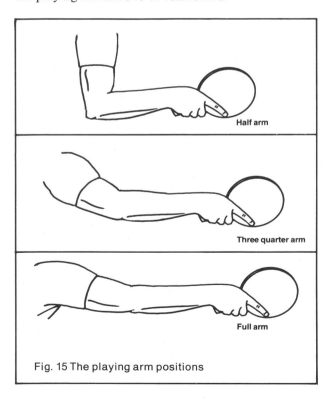

Fig. 15 The playing arm positions

22

Free arm

A player needs to play strokes co-ordinating the whole of the body, not just using the playing arm which would make him a powerless, one-sided player. Because you need to play with the whole of the body, it is important that the non-playing arm (free arm) is incorporated into all strokes. This will have an influence on your performance on three counts:

1 The power to the stroke
2 Balance when playing a stroke
3 Balance when recovering after playing a stroke

This type of movement is impossible to perform if the free hand is not used to give effective weight transference and stabilisation to the stroke. This also applies to the recovery back to a ready position in preparing for the next stroke.

You need to make full use of the body and to pivot from the waist to produce power for a stroke. The position of the free arm should correspond to that of the playing arm, so that the movement of the free arm is similar to that of the playing arm, to fit the movement of the stroke (Fig. 16A). All strokes cannot be played from a stable position – use your free arm to help (Fig. 16B).

If you are playing a short or a medium form stroke, then the free arm should be relatively close to the side of the body, at an angle of about 90 degrees, letting the body move freely. If the stroke is long and dynamic then you need to make full use of the leverage that can be made – from 120 to 180 degrees in the execution of the stroke.

Fig. 16A Effective use of the free arm

Fig. 16B Free arm helps in an unstable position

Chapter 2 **Use of spin**

Spin plays a major role in the game today. There are three main variations to be used according to the tactical demands:

1 *Control spin*
   To be used when your opponent makes a good return, which cannot be attacked.
2 *Deception*
   Use deception, particularly with service, but also with the strokes you return. If your opponent is deceived as to the amount of spin that has been applied to the ball, he may make a mistake and be forced to play the ball into the net, off the end of the table, or to give a high return so that the ball can then be smashed.
3 *Power spin*
   This mainly applies to the topspin player who imparts excessive spin to the ball from his speedy, dynamic, actions. Excessive spin can also be a weapon used by the backspin style player.

As you see, spin is a very important weapon which can be used in many ways, so it is important that you know the mechanics of spin for both receiving and applying it. A question I often ask both players and coaches is, 'How do you apply spin?' Their stock reply is, 'The angle and the contact of the racquet on the ball.' However, that is not quite correct – that is the end product. It is a combination of speed of movement in the arms and body that creates power, plus taction (touch). The more lightly you can touch or brush the ball with the racquet, at speed, the greater the amount of spin will be imparted. This is one of the reasons why the inverted rubber racquet produces more spin, as there are no restrictions on the playing surface.

Topspin

Topspin can be applied from a stroke that goes in an upward or a forward movement, rotating the ball as in Fig. 17. The contact point on the ball when playing a topspin will be a governing factor on:

1 The amount of spin applied to the ball
2 The speed at which the ball travels
3 The trajectory of the ball

For example, if you use the contact point in Fig. 18 this would give a spin plus speed return, with the trajectory of the ball keeping relatively low on the opponent's side of the table. The contact point in Fig. 19 is an advancement on the one in Fig.18 and could be used as a variation. The effect that the stroke would have on the ball would be that of speed plus spin and the trajectory of the ball would keep low.

On the third type of topspin going in a vertical direction, the emphasis would be on spin (Fig. 20).

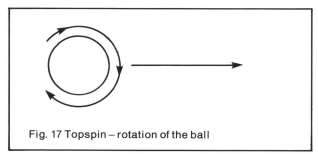

Fig. 17 Topspin – rotation of the ball

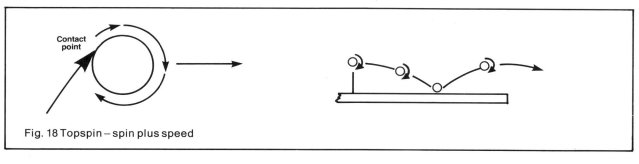

Fig. 18 Topspin – spin plus speed

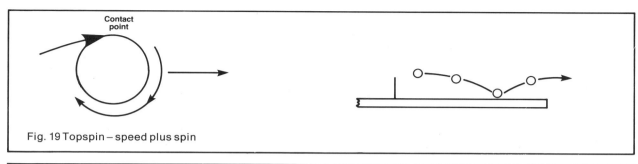

Fig. 19 Topspin – speed plus spin

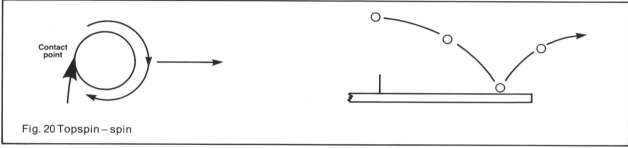

Fig. 20 Topspin – spin

As you see, the varying contact points on the ball will give you different speeds, spins and trajectories, to be used as part of your strategy. Remember, if you have only one type of topspin then your opponent will soon be used to your returns whereas, if you use more than one, he will have to wait until you play the ball before knowing which type you have used.

Backspin

Backspin can be thought of as the reverse of topspin.

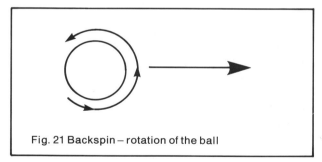

Fig. 21 Backspin – rotation of the ball

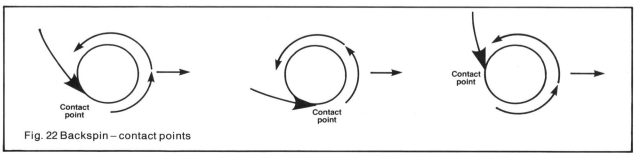

Fig. 22 Backspin – contact points

25

That is, you would start the stroke above or behind the ball, going in a forward or downward movement (Fig. 21).

Just as there are three contact points for topspin there are also three contact points for backspin (Fig. 22). Each contact point will have its own characteristics in spin. All the returns are relatively slow. The object when playing a backspin is to keep the ball as low as possible and to vary the amount of spin applied to the ball.

Float

This type of return puts the minimum amount of spin on the ball and could have a small amount of either topspin or backspin, depending on where the stroke starts. If you started your stroke either above or behind the ball, but instead of brushing the ball as lightly as possible to apply spin, you made greater contact on the ball, it would give relatively little spin. One of the arts of deception is to develop a stroke so that the same movements are applied for both spin and float, thus making the amount of spin applied to the ball difficult for your opponent to read, leading him to make a mistake with his returns.

Sidespin

Sidespin is applied by brushing the racquet as lightly as possible across the ball, but this is seldom used except when serving. It is more commonly used in stroke play and service by incorporating topspin and sidespin or backspin and sidespin (Fig. 23).

Some players have the ability to spin the ball with ease, others will find it more difficult. If you find it hard to spin the ball do not despair; the drive type of game also has its advantages. I think at this point that we need to clear up a few fallacies. Some players and coaches believe that when a player plays a loop stroke (topspin) the aim is to keep the ball on the racquet as long as possible, and that the ball runs up the racquet. This is not so – the time that the ball is in contact with the racquet is the same for loop strokes as it is for a push or smash stroke. It is the friction between ball and racquet and the contact point which produces spin. For a topspin stroke you will use the lower part of the racquet rather than the

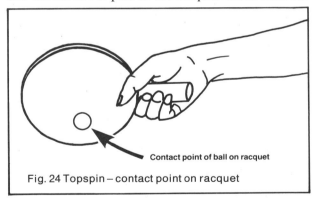
Fig. 24 Topspin – contact point on racquet
Contact point of ball on racquet

centre (Fig. 24). You will find that the outer part of the racquet can produce greater spin than the inner part and this should be used when playing a topspin and also when serving. On some types of service the outer part of the racquet is travelling fastest and the inner part barely travels at all. The inner part of the racquet could be used, for example, for a control push, backspin (chop), hit or smash.

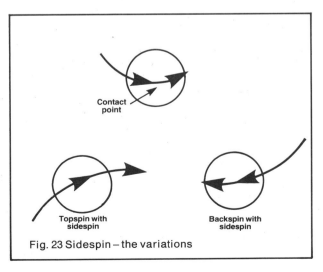
Contact point
Topspin with sidespin
Backspin with sidespin
Fig. 23 Sidespin – the variations

Chapter 3 Practice

A successful player is one who can execute a skilled action and also the one who has sound basic technique when playing strokes. He will be able to perform skilled techniques in the various situations met during practice and competition. Having good technique in stroke play is dependent on having the co-ordination necessary for specific movements. To be able consistently to perform good technique, it is important to spend a great deal of time practising and building up a series of movement patterns until they become habitual. The conditioning of these movement patterns is one of the most important factors in skill learning, as it will help you to acquire well-timed muscular co-ordination, vital in competitive situations. When developing a particular technique there are certain aspects of these competitive situations which you should consider. You will receive a constantly changing variety of return, such as a ball with very little spin; a ball with excessive spin; a ball with no spin or a ball received at speed. These returns will be received from varying angles of the table.

With this in mind, the practice stimulus used should be specific to the technique required. This applies not only to the movement pattern involved but also to the speed of movement, the force exerted and the amount of taction (touch) required. The correct interaction between movement, speed, force and taction, is necessary to obtain optimal results. Although developing a specific technique requires these four components, they should not be thought of as separate entities, but should be developed together.

In spite of the saying, practice does not always make perfect. Practice needs to be based upon intelligent, organised planning, taking the following factors into consideration:

1   The length of the practice session
2   The complexity of the skill
3   The mental and physical application required for each skill practice
4   The work/rest ratio of a given skill practice

When organising practices it is important to divide the practice time so that everyone involved knows what they are going to do and what they have to achieve from the practice session. It could be grooving a stroke by using stability play, or improving footwork by movements from side to side, or developing new service techniques. There are many aspects of the game to be practised – remember to practise your strong points as well as your weak ones.

Lines of play
Each time you practise you should use a particular line of play – this could be diagonal or straight (Fig. 25) and it is important to remember when playing on a specific line that your stance is to that line of play and not to the table.

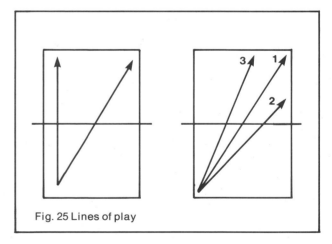

Fig. 25 Lines of play

The *diagonal* is the longest line of play and can be used in three different ways:
1   Playing on the diagonal
2   Playing diagonally with the ball going off the side line
3   Playing diagonally with the ball going off the end line

The *straight* is to play parallel to the length of the table.

Areas of play

When practising, as well as using lines of play you should also use an area of play (Fig. 26). When you are

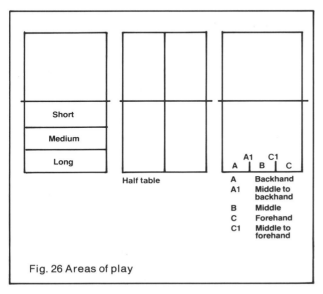

Fig. 26 Areas of play

proficient at playing to these areas consistently you should reduce the area accordingly. In practices you should not think of success as merely playing the ball on the table. You are only successful if you play the ball on the specific line and in the area intended. Do not, however, impair the quality of the stroke in order to hit a particular part of the table.

When organising a specific practice period you can work to a set time or to a number of repetitions.

Practice periods using time

In first learning a particular stroke, you can practise for 10 to 15 minutes and as you become more proficient the practice can be extended. This length of practice period would be used for a practice which is not too strenuous, such as stability practice but a more strenuous practice of footwork might only last for 10 minutes, depending on the amount of physical exertion needed.

Practice periods using number of repetitions

Practice by using a number of repetitions could be used for consistency practice. You could set a number of strokes to play without making a mistake – choose, for example, 40 slow forehand drives – if a mistake is made on the 25th stroke, then you have to go back to zero. If you achieve the 40 strokes without a mistake then you could add another 10 strokes and so on. The Japanese players on their National Training Camps have to play **1000** strokes without making a mistake. When using this type of play you should always see that there is quality in the stroke and good placing of the ball. Consistency is only one feature of play and only one step towards being a good player – what counts in the end is the effectiveness of your strokes in winning points.

Another way of using 'numbers' or 'repetitions' is in improving your service. You could practise one particular service and use 100 repetitions. If you are lucky enough to have 100 balls at your disposal, you could serve 100 balls. This type of practice does not require an opponent on the other side of the table. Under these conditions you will be able to spend some time thinking and experimenting.

Practice periods are used to develop not only stroke but also mental and physical application. You need mental application to be able to read your opponent's game and physical application to achieve the dynamic or sustained movements demanded.

After each practice, whether using the time or the number of repetitions method, you need to rest. It is important to have a good work/rest ratio. It is pointless to practise while mentally or physically fatigued. If you are tired, take a five minute break and then resume the practice.

In the early stages of learning a stroke, it may be convenient to isolate a skill so that improvement can be made. It is of equal importance to be aware of the context into which this skill must fit. By keeping the skill in isolation the process of learning and the development of tactical awareness will be retarded.

Speed of play

Table tennis is a game of speeds and spins. The speed of the ball can be slow, medium or fast and when practising the strokes, the various speeds should be introduced. It is an essential part of a player's strategy to be able to vary and control the speed of play. Practise first of all 40 slow backhand drives, 20 medium and 10 fast. Then play for a period of 10, 15 or 20 minutes and vary the speed – play a slow return then fast, then slow, then medium and so on. It is important not to become a one speed player.

Stability practice

Repetitious or stability practice is a way of grooving strokes and developing stability within a stroke. Problems that can develop with this type of practice are that the player's stance (the position to the line of play) the speed and spin of the ball and also the direction in which the ball is travelling, are all pre-dictable. These can in many ways be the deciding factors between winning and losing. A player will be able to play a stroke well from a static point, but he must also develop good anticipation and tactical awareness.

Therefore, practice needs to be divided further into two categories:

1   Practice with co-operation from the opponent
2   Practice with opposition from the opponent

Practice with co-operation is important when a player is learning a stroke. Co-operation will allow rhythmic, co-ordinated movement to develop between player and opponent. After the stroke has been practised and grooved, it is important to break this co-operative attitude and to introduce the element of opposition.

Remember that all practice is simulated, therefore all practice needs to be developed in stages and once a player reaches a particular point in learning a skill, progression and advancement need to be made. One of the most difficult factors to deal with in a competition is stress. This cannot be simulated in practices and you can only learn how to deal with it in competitive situations.

Footwork

During the course of a game you have to move in different directions. This movement may be slow and sustained or fast and explosive – depending upon the relative strength of the balls received and the stroke about to be played. Footwork and fitness are closely related; the player needs strength and speed to create the power for the dynamic and explosive movements which have to be made. It is not only the movements that are important but also the player's ability to organise and react so as to be in position to play the required stroke. The main source of power is in the legs, and the combination of strength and speed will develop the power for the movement required. Effective weight transference will also result in a more powerful stroke. There are two types of footwork – stepping and running.

Stepping footwork

Stepping footwork is used mainly by the player who plays close to the table, such as the drive-style player or the blocker. It could also be used by players with good anticipation, who position themselves so well that they only have to take one or two steps to play their stroke, or if the play is concentrated within a small area of the table (Fig. 27). From a ready position step with the foot nearer the ball then play your stroke.

Running footwork

This type of footwork is used mainly by players who play away from the table and who have to move over a large area when playing their strokes, for example, topspin, backspin and drive players. A high level of fitness is required if a player has to rely on this type of footwork (Fig. 28). You may need to use large strides and then smaller movements to adjust, to enable you to play your stroke.

All players will make use of both types of foot-work at some time during a game. The extent to which each is used depends upon your own style of play and your opponent's. If a backspin player is playing a top-spin player, who is only playing deep topspins down

29

Fig. 27 Stepping footwork

one wing (all returns down the backspin player's forehand) then the backspin player may use 80 per cent stepping footwork and 20 per cent running footwork. But if the topspin player plays down both wings (returns down both backhand and forehand) and also incorporates drop shots, then the percentage of footwork could change to 80 per cent running footwork and 20 per cent stepping footwork. As you can see, the degree of fitness required will fluctuate, depending upon the style of player. The second type of backspin player needs to be much fitter and to have greater endurance than the first type of player.

30

Fig. 28A

Fig. 28B

Fig. 28C

Fig. 28D

Fig. 28E

Fig. 28 Running footwork

31

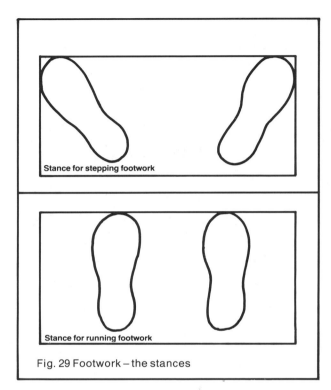

Fig. 29 Footwork – the stances

The stance and foot positioning differ according to the style of footwork used. A player who 'steps' and plays close to the table will have a wider stance and the feet will be spread a little more than those of the player who 'runs'. The latter will have a narrower stance, with the feet positioned at a less acute angle (Fig. 29). Footwork practice requires movement side to side and in and out, or a combination of both. When practising footwork, there are two types: regular and irregular.

Regular footwork

This type of footwork is used to practise a new movement and also to develop rhythm, by playing the ball from different positions on the table in a uniform pattern. This type of practice is predictable and should be kept to a minimum.

Irregular footwork

Irregular footwork will be used when the ball is played in no particular order or sequence. This will introduce unpredictability and the competitive element into the practice, and decisions will have to be made. Irregular footwork not only improves a player's footwork but also helps a player to read various match situations and develops anticipation. When practising footwork, as with all practices, start with co-operation and later introduce opposition, in this case by increasing the speed of play.

Stroke practice

A stroke needs to be built up in three phases and should be introduced in this sequence:

Phase 1, Stability practice

The first phase of developing a new stroke technique is to build a controlled, rhythmic, co-ordinated movement, using arms, body and feet with dexterity. Control and consistency should be practised until the movements become automatic.

Phase 2, Footwork

The second phase is to introduce movement around the various parts of the table, again with controlled, rhythmic, co-ordinated movements. Various types of footwork should be used, either in and out or side to side.

Phase 3, Point winning

Phase 3 involves playing and combining strokes into point winning sequences and knowing which stroke to play in any situation, such as a third and fifth or fourth and sixth ball attack.

The stroke practices and sequences that are in the following chapters are simple to follow and include the various strokes needed for specific styles of play. To miss out any of these could leave a weak area in your game. Avoid devoting a whole practice session to one stroke; preferably use two to start with and then build up. When practising Phase 3 blend the strokes around the strongest stroke.

Chapter 4 Stroke play

Offensive or defensive

When we think of different styles of play, we think of attacking play and defensive play. We think of a defensive player as a backspin style player and an attacking player as a drive or topspin style player, but are we correct to assume this? One could hardly say that backspin players such as Liang Geliang Takashima, or Jill Hammersley are defensive players. On the contrary, on many occasions it is their opponents who are on the defensive. In many styles played today there is also the topspin style of defence as well as the backspin. When we think of a stroke we should think of it in two contexts: *offensive* and *defensive*. All the strokes that you use should be thought of and learned in this way; from the simple push to the complex topspin. There will be times when the ball received can be attacked and also times when caution will have to take priority, and then you will have to go on the defensive. I like to think in terms of a player controlling play rather than defending. Play is controlled until the opportunity can be seized to go on the offensive. In competition you cannot take the initiative all the time; if you cannot attack the first ball then you should try to attack the next. *The best form of defence is attack*.

Middle game

There are certain strokes that are required in every player's repertoire whether a topspin or backspin style player. These are *hitting (drive)*, *smash*, *block*, *push*, *drop shot*, with both the backhand and the forehand. The drive and the smash will be covered later in the book but let us look first of all at the *block, push* and *drop shot* strokes. These are played mainly close to, or over the table. Many players call this the *middle game* as these strokes are played when a player is not able to drive, topspin, or backspin the ball, depending upon the style of play. Some ill-informed players will say that they never push a ball. This cannot be correct as a player will not always receive a ball that he can drive, topspin or backspin. What you must remember is that you can counter the many varied types of spin and speed received on the ball by using the push and the block with the correct racquet angle and the right amount of taction and dexterity.

Block

The *block* stroke can be used both as a *control* or *attacking* stroke. It can be used to take your opponent in and out from the table, or to stretch him wide from side to side. It is also a stroke that is mainly used against a ball which has been played with topspin, or a ball which has been hit or smashed. But it would not be used against a backspin ball.

If the block is used as a *control* stroke, you would neutralise the spin and the speed from the ball received from your opponent, producing a cushioning effect between the racquet and the ball, by relaxing the grip, the wrist and the arm. If an *attacking* return is used the player should make use of the opponent's spin and speed. The grip and wrist would be much firmer and the movement from the arm much quicker, making use of the fast moving joints in the arm (elbow, wrist). The stance should be square with a good solid base when playing the stroke, with the timing between early to peak of bounce (you would not block on a late timing) (Figs. 30 and 31).

For the forehand block use a side stance with your arm at 90 degrees at the elbow for good control. Apply the appropriate racquet angle to meet the spin and speed of the ball received.

In addition to the control and attacking block, there is a third type: *a block with backspin*. This can be used as a variation especially against a ball with a small amount of topspin, or a medium hit ball (Fig. 32). The principles are as for the backhand block but with a downward not a forward movement.

Push

The push stroke will mainly be played against a backspin return, or a relatively slow ball. The same principles apply to the push as for the block, but the governing factor will be the racquet angle. For a push stroke the racquet angle is open in contrast to the

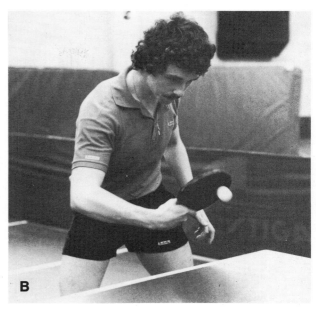

Fig. 30 Backhand block

Stellan Bengtsson tries to keep his eye on the ball

closed angle of the block. It would be unwise to think of pushing close to the table a ball that had heavy top-spin or a ball that was travelling at speed. It would be more advantageous to use a block. Again, the *push* can be used as a *control* or *attacking* stroke. If you are using a control stroke, you should use the centre of the racquet, but if it is an attacking stroke, you can use the outer part of the racquet. If the outer part of the racquet is used you can apply more spin and, if desired, speed. To achieve this you would have to use a relaxed and flexible wrist to allow fast movement. A ball that has been pushed will vary from a ball with a small amount of backspin (float) to a heavily chopped ball.

When playing a backhand push, play from a square stance with the movement from the elbow going in an upward direction (Fig. 33). For the fore-hand push, move from the ready position into a side stance and with a combined movement from elbow and shoulder play the ball in a forward motion (Fig. 34). For both backhand and forehand strokes you

35

Fig. 31 Forehand block

Fig. 32 Backhand block with backspin

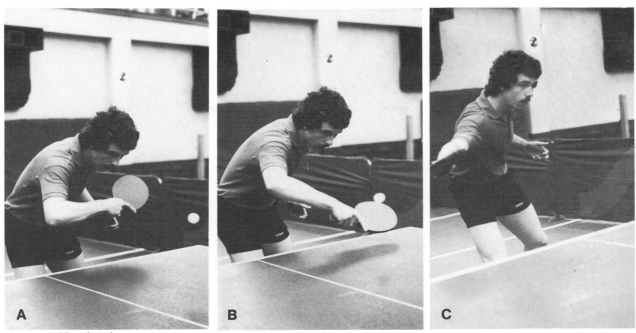

Fig. 33 Backhand push

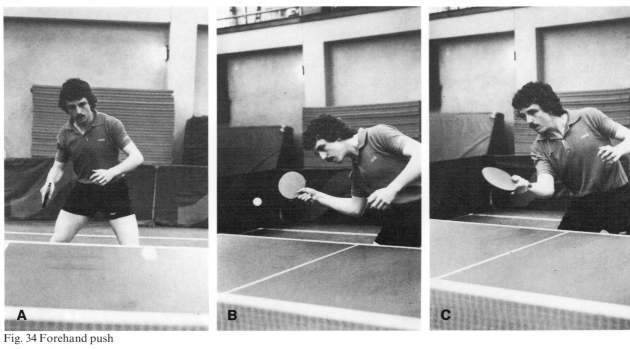

Fig. 34 Forehand push

should chop over the table brushing the ball lightly.
Drop shot
Both drive and topspin players should master this stroke to use mainly against backspin players. It can be used in two ways. Firstly, as I said earlier, you cannot attack every ball but you can use the drop shot to break up the game against a backspin player. Secondly, if you cannot penetrate the backspin player's game with your forehand drive or topspin, you could use a short drop shot (just over the net) on the middle to forehand or backhand side of your opponent's side of the table. You should try to use the drop shot then play a topspin or drive, mixing the returns and forcing the backspin player to make a mistake by bringing him forwards and backwards or moving him from side to side, whichever is the weaker movement, or by using a combination of both ploys. If you are successful with the drop shot it will be an advantage when receiving a short service which needs to be returned short.

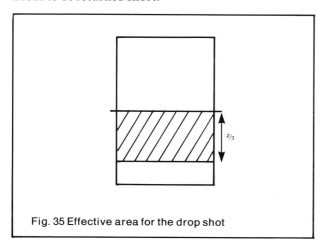

Fig. 35 Effective area for the drop shot

The main feature of the drop shot is that it is most effective when your opponent plays a shot within the area shown in Fig. 35. It is difficult to play this stroke if the return from your opponent is deep, as the main aim is to play the ball just over the net, and to make it

bounce at least twice on your opponent's side of the table. You should try to play the stroke early, just after the bounce of the ball, and you will have to read the spin on the ball so that you can use the correct racquet angle. The racquet angle will be open, the grip will be more relaxed than usual, and there should be minimal forward movement to the stroke. If there is forward movement or the racquet is held firmly the ball will rebound and will go deeper into your opponent's court and he could then attack.

As this is a control stroke it is important that the arm angle is at 90 degrees and that the player is close to the ball. It can also be effective when playing against topspin players – the racquet at this time would have a closed angle. Again, it is important to read the spin and to use the relevant racquet angle to counteract it (Fig. 36).

Tactically, the drop shot can be used to surprise all styles of player, but it needs to be applied with dexterity and when least expected.

Practice for middle game, all players
Phase 1
Practice for: stability play, grooving strokes, control over movements, control over ball, touch play.

Stability play is for two players to practise on one line of play. Each player will be grooving his strokes and movements; only a minimal amount of positional movement will be necessary during this type of practice. The only movement will be a small adjustment of the feet to allow each player to be in position to play his stroke. Consistency will be included to see how many strokes can be played without making a mistake. Control over the ball needs also to be practised and the ball is played where the player intends it to go, with the right amount of touch.
Phase 2
Practice for: regular footwork, varying timing.

Practise regular footwork using stepping sideways. When varying timing use also in and out footwork. Use both backhand and forehand.

Anneli Hernvall prepares to play a forehand loop

Fig. 36 Drop shot

One player should control while the other practises footwork and varying timing on the in and out exercises. Remember to practise all these exercises at varying speeds, playing slow, medium and fast. On the footwork exercises, first use regular footwork practice and then move on to irregular footwork. Practise in two contexts – control and attack.

Phase 3

Competition practice.

This will be covered in the other practice sections as you would mainly combine the push with other strokes in a competitive situation. The practices for the block can be seen in the practice for the topspin and drive shots and the drop shot in the section on backspin.

Practices for middle game are on page 41.

Abbreviations for middle game practices

F.H.P.	Forehand push
B.H.P.	Backhand push
R.V.P.	Reverse practice

Practices for middle game
Phase1

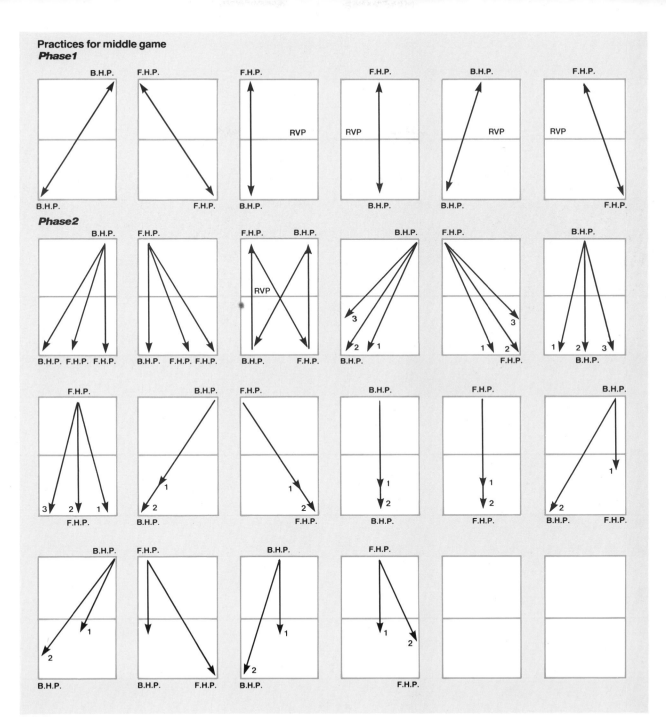

Phase2

Chapter 5 Topspin style of game

The topspin style of game is one of the most popular in the sport today. The amount of spin that is applied to the ball has reached new boundaries, thanks to the science that has been used in developing the rubbers and racquets, the technology applied by the trainers and coaches, and last but not least, the dynamic athleticism employed by players in the execution of these strokes.

The topspin stroke called the *loop* is a stroke which produces a greater amount of topspin, and was developed by the Japanese in the mid-Fifties. Between the mid-Fifties and early Seventies the loop was played mainly with a vertical stroke with the emphasis upon producing increased spin, but in today's game the emphasis is more upon the power spin which was introduced by the Hungarians, making them both European and World Men's Team Champions, ousting the Chinese domination of the men's team event.

What is required to be a looper?
1 Height, to provide the necessary leverage
2 Skill in the technique of spinning the ball
3 A high level of co-ordination of arms, legs and body
4 Dexterity and the ability to apply varying degrees of taction to the ball
5 Strength in all parts of the body
6 Power and speed of movement to play the stroke efficiently

Topspin technique

The topspin player has a variety of techniques to learn. Topspin shots can be fast, slow, long, short, or with added sidespin. Some players are able to develop up to four different types of topspin strokes. There are, however, improved techniques to provide an effective response to topspin strokes, so even if your topspin is quite powerful and used consistently, it cannot be guaranteed that you will win the point. Because of this, you should try to use at least two types of topspin loop techniques during a game. If you can use a long,

fast topspin and also a slow, high topspin it will be to your advantage. The combination of these two types of topspin can be quite effective, each helping the other because of the spin applied, the flight of the ball and also the variation in pace.

Power topspin loop, fast and low

The power topspin loop that is played fast and low is played with a fast and powerful forward motion. One of the key factors when playing this stroke is the base of the player. This should be stable and a good side stance should be adopted enabling the player to transfer his weight through in a forward motion. The ball should be played at the peak of the bounce, the playing arm should be at 120 degrees for good leverage, and as the weight is transferred forward, the ball is brushed as fast as possible before the player resumes the ready position (Fig. 37).

In the section on spin I described two contact points on the ball. For the power loop the second (Fig. 19 page 25) will give a faster return with a great deal of spin. A finer degree of timing is required and for maximum effect the arm angle should be around 160 degrees when playing this stroke.

For the forehand loop with emphasis on speed and spin the racquet is held much higher than for the forehand loop, spin and speed. Note also that the free and playing arms are at 160 degrees, with a powerful forward movement producing speed and spin before recovery back to the ready position (Fig. 38).

Topspin loop, slow and high

The slow, high topspin loop is still an effective stroke with the emphasis upon increased topspin. It is especially effective if played just over the net (short) on your opponent's forehand or if played against penhold players deep into their backhand. It will be difficult for this return to be played and controlled by a penhold player playing a backhand, as the ball will bounce too high with a lot of spin to allow an effective block to be played. The slow, high topspin loop is more

Jill Hammersley attacking with a backspin stroke

44   Fig. 37 Forehand loop; spin and speed

Fig. 38 Forehand loop; speed and spin

Page 46 Guo Yuehua demonstrates a high service

Fig. 39 Forehand high loop; spin

effective if the arm angle is at 90 degrees to the elbow. Unlike the power loop, where the power is in a forward motion, the power for this stroke is in a vertical direction, with the preparation for the stroke lower than that for the power loop. The ball will also be played on a later timing. From the ready position move into a side stance; note the low position of the racquet. The weight is transferred vertically and with a fast movement before recovering into the ready position (Fig. 39).

Backhand loop

It is important to have a two wing attack. You will need an effective backhand as well as a forehand, so that you can open the attack or win a point with either stroke.

The backhand loop follows the same principle as the forehand – the strokes are played in the same direction and using the same contact points. However, unlike the forehand, the backhand makes use of the power from the elbow and especially the wrist (Fig. 40). From the ready position move into a square

Fig. 40 Backhand loop – note wrist position

48

Page 47 Dragutin Surbek shows the need for good footwork

Fig. 41 Backhand loop

stance; the wrist should be low to give extra speed to the movement. Note the racquet angle. The racquet moves through 180 degrees by a powerful forward movement from the wrist and elbow (Fig. 41).

Practice for the topspin game
Phase 1
Practice for: stability play, grooving strokes, control over movements, control over ball, touch play.

Stability play, grooving strokes and control over movements are all covered in these practices as in the practices for the middle game. The difference here is that player A will be practising topspin whilst player B will be practising the block. Player A's aim is to control the ball and apply the correct amount of touch, imparting varying degrees of spin, first using the slow, high loop then moving on to the two power loops that are fast and low. Player B aims to control the spin.

Phase 2
Practice for: regular footwork, varying timing.

Both players can organise their practice so that regular footwork exercises can be used. All that is required for you to do is to reverse the exercises. Remember that for the fast loops the timing point can

be at peak of bounce or early and that the slow loop is played mainly on a late timing. For the block, use peak of the bounce or an early timing depending upon the amount of spin imparted.

Phase 3
Practice for: point winning ploys.

When practising ploys, on no account should your practice opponent co-operate with you, giving you an easy ball to play. A match situation should be simulated as far as possible.

Practices for topspin game are on pages 50 and 51.

Abbreviations for topspin practices

F.H.T.S.	Forehand topspin
B.H.T.S.	Backhand topspin
F.H.B.	Forehand block
B.H.B.	Backhand block
F.S.H.L.	Forehand slow high loop
F.F.L.L.	Forehand fast low loop
B.S.H.L.	Backhand slow high loop
F.H.D.	Forehand drive
S.H.L.	Slow high loop

Practices for topspin game
Phase1

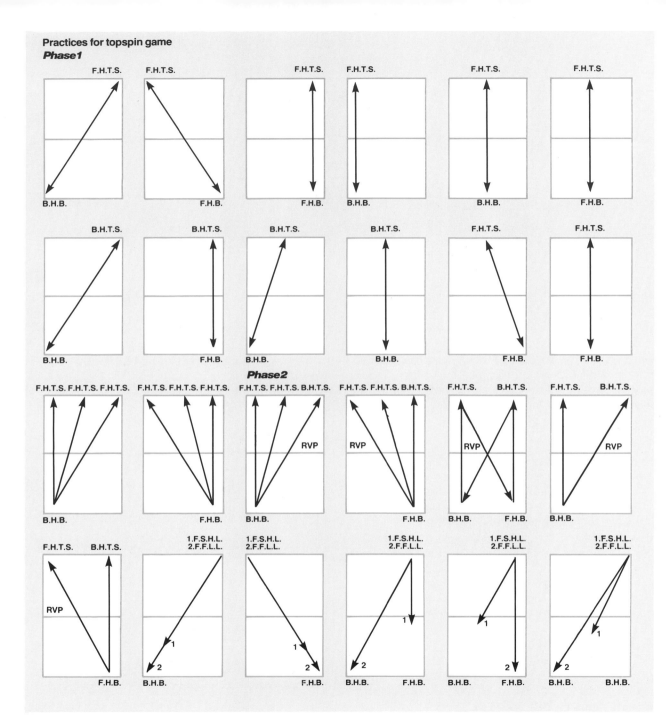

Phase2

Practices for topspin game continued
Phase 3

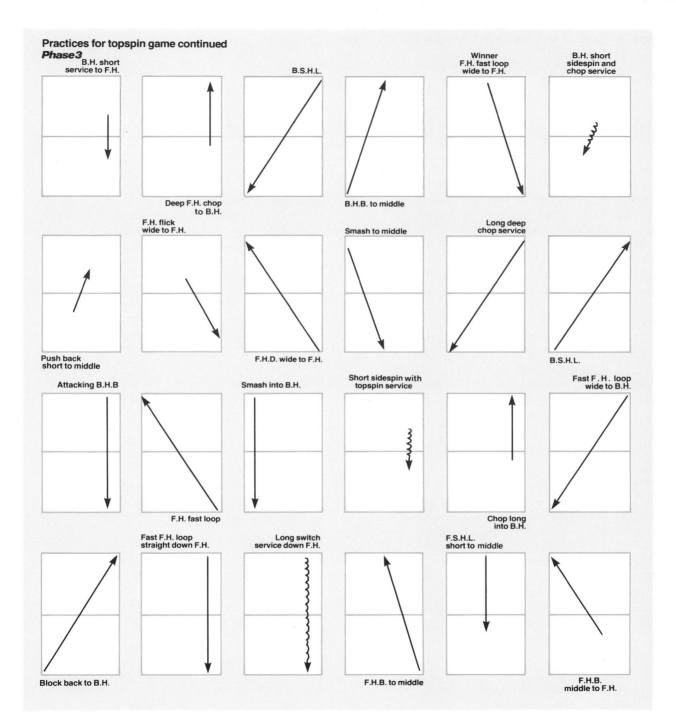

B.H. short service to F.H.

B.S.H.L.

Winner F.H. fast loop wide to F.H.

B.H. short sidespin and chop service

Deep F.H. chop to B.H.

B.H.B. to middle

F.H. flick wide to F.H.

Smash to middle

Long deep chop service

Push back short to middle

F.H.D. wide to F.H.

B.S.H.L.

Attacking B.H.B

Smash into B.H.

Short sidespin with topspin service

Fast F.H. loop wide to B.H.

F.H. fast loop

Chop long into B.H.

Fast F.H. loop straight down F.H.

Long switch service down F.H.

F.S.H.L. short to middle

Block back to B.H.

F.H.B. to middle

F.H.B. middle to F.H.

51

Chapter 6 Backspin style of game

The backspin style of game has increased in popularity in recent years with the introduction of the *anti-loop rubber* and many varieties of long pimple rubbers, together with the defensive racquet blades. In the past, the materials manufactured favoured the topspin and drive player, but many successful players such as Kreisz of Hungary, Huging of Federal Germany and John Hilton of England, not to mention the numerous Chinese players, owe much of their success to the type and combination of rubbers used. There are pundits who refer to these players as *material players* and say that they would not be successful without this type of rubber, but this same argument could also apply to the powerful looper or the speedy drive player, who could not spin or drive the ball so hard if it were not for the type of materials they use. I will discuss the combination player at the end of this section. The requirements for a backspin player are as follows:

1 A high level of skill
2 Hand/eye co-ordination
3 Dexterity in varying the taction
4 Fitness and endurance
5 Strength in all parts of the body

Backspin technique

The basic requirement of a topspin player, to be able to use varying types of spin, also applies to the backspin player. You need to be able to vary the amount of spin from a floating ball (minimal spin) to one with a high degree of backspin. This should be achieved by using the same type of stroke, in particular using the same motion, thus making it more difficult for your opponent to read your moves. Against an experienced player more points can be won by forcing him into an error through deception than by trying to break down his consistency. Backspin play can be played in three areas of the table:

1 Over the table
2 At the end of the table (mid-section)
3 Away from the table

The backspin player, like the topspin player, has to be strong on both wings (backhand and forehand) and also needs to be able to use various timings and contact points on the ball to counter the various returns he will receive. Let us first look at the backhand chop.

Backhand backspin (chop)

There are two stances that can be used when playing a backhand chop: the square stance and the side stance. Each type of stance has its merits and both stances should be practised.

Square stance

The square stance can be used against any type of return and also on any timing, with the exception of a very late timing. It can also be played in any of the three areas of the table that we spoke about earlier. One of the main advantages of using a square stance is that your return will be more controlled and the placement of the ball on your opponent's side of the table is usually more accurate. When playing a chop from the square stance position, the stroke is played at the left side of the body (for the right hander) and not in the centre of the body as many coaches and players think. One of the principles of the backhand chop from the square stance is that the stroke is played mainly from the elbow with the shoulder and wrist as secondary movers. (See also Fig. 33.)

If the stroke is played from the centre of the body then the elbow has to move out and this will restrict movement and limit control from the elbow. Do not adopt a square stance if playing a stroke on a very late timing or if the ball has been played wide to the backhand.

Side stance

For the backhand backspin, adopt a side stance, take the weight on the back leg, take the racquet back and play the stroke down and forward brushing the ball lightly but with a fast movement (Fig. 42).

Fig. 42 Backhand backspin

Fig. 43 Forehand backspin (chop)

Fig. 44 A variation on forehand backspin

Side stance

The advantage in playing a stroke from a side stance is that your weight can be transferred in two directions, that is, either forwards or sideways. With the square stance, only forward weight transference is advisable.

Remember when playing against a powerful top-spin player to let the spin on the ball die by playing the stroke on a very late timing. This will make the return much easier to control.

Forehand backspin (chop)

The same principles apply for the forehand as for the backhand. The backhand stroke, especially the one from a square stance, is played mainly from the elbow, but with the forehand, the stroke will mainly be played from the shoulder, especially when away from the table. When the stroke is played close to or over the table, the elbow and wrist could be used for faster and more efficient movement.

As in Fig. 43, move from the ready position into a side stance, note the racquet angle and use a whipping action from the wrist to give varying spins. As a variation, take the weight on the back leg and instead of transferring the weight forward, transfer sideways (Fig. 44). This would be used on a late timing against a fast or heavily spun ball.

Backspin can be useful for a topspin or a drive player to use when driven away from the table and the opponent is on the offensive with strong returns. To play the occasional heavy chop may throw your opponent onto the defensive where he may use a control topspin, thus allowing you to take the initiative and go on the offensive.

Practice for the backspin game
Phase 1
Practice for: stability play, grooving strokes, control over movements, control over ball, touch play.

55

Stability play, grooving strokes, control over movements apply to these practices as for middle game and topspin practices. The difference here is that player A will be practising backspin while player B will be practising topspin. Both players need to pay particular attention to the varying amounts of spin that their practice partner is applying to the ball, and after reading this they should dextrously apply the correct amount of touch to their strokes.

Phase 2

Practice for: regular footwork, varying timing.

Again both players can organise the practice so that regular footwork can be used. The backspin player should practise playing the ball on varying timings, but remember not to chop a ball with heavy topspin on an early timing; only a ball with a minimal amount of topspin should be chopped over the table.

When practising backspin remember to mix a floating ball along with the variation in chop – it can be a winner.

Phase 3

Practice for: point winning.

The main way for a backspin player to win is by deception. This will be done by varying the type and amount of spin on the ball, and also by moving the opponent about. If you play to one position then your opponent could get used to it. Remember to break up the game by using the third ball attack.

Abbreviations for backspin practices
F.H.B.S.   Forehand backspin
B.H.B.S.   Backhand backspin
F.H.T.S.   Forehand topspin
B.H.T.S.   Backhand topspin
R.V.P.   Reverse practice

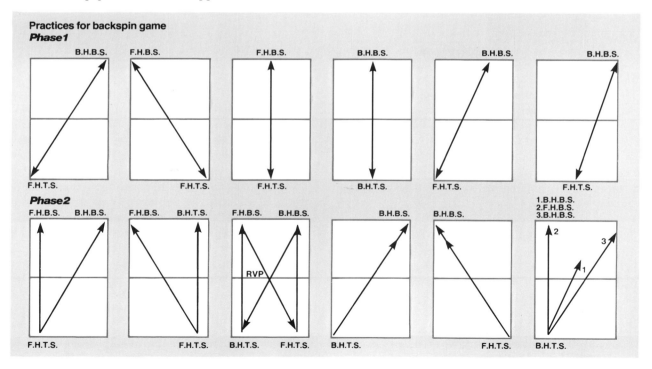

Chapter 7 Drive style of game

The drive style of game can be divided into two categories. The first type is where the player will mainly use forehand and backhand drive strokes with the added block on both wings, and the second type is to drive on the forehand only and block on the backhand. With the latter style, the player will mainly drive with the forehand and block with the backhand. The former style can be played close to, or at middle distance from the table, but the second type will inevitably be played close to the table and will not be effective away from the table. The drive style player will try to win points early in a rally with an attack on the third and fifth or fourth and sixth ball. (See also Chapter 11.)

The requirements for a drive style player are:
1 A high level of skill
2 A high level of multi-body co-ordination
3 Dexterity, especially in the wrist, to facilitate constant change of racquet angle
4 Good reflex actions to cope with the speed of play
5 The ability to organise quickly
6 Power for explosive movement

Drive technique

In skill learning there is a lot of talk about abilities; about having ball sense, about having an eye for the ball, and so on. There are, of course, players who have a good eye for the ball but who are unable to spin the ball effectively. This type of player could well be a drive style player. The game is basically the same as the topspin game but instead of winning points by spinning the ball points are won by speed, and by hitting through the ball. All drive strokes should go in a forward motion, especially if playing against a fellow drive style player or a topspin player. Against a backspin player the stroke may need to go in a more vertical direction to counter the backspin.

The block stroke has been covered in Chapter 4, so I will now move on to the drive stroke and the smash.

Forehand drive

The forehand drive is a power stroke that needs to go in a forward direction. The power for this stroke comes mainly from the upper part of the body, by rotating from the trunk and using a fast co-ordinated

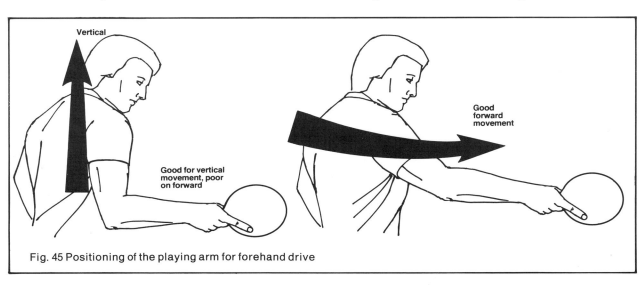

Vertical

Good for vertical movement, poor on forward

Good forward movement

Fig. 45 Positioning of the playing arm for forehand drive

Fig. 46A

Fig. 46B

Fig. 46C

Fig. 46D

Fig. 46E

Fig. 46 Forehand drive

movement from the playing arm. When talking about a fast movement from the playing arm it is important to ensure that the power and efficiency of the movement are correct. Power and efficiency will be lost if the playing arm is incorrectly positioned.

In drive play, the ball should be taken at the peak of the bounce. If your elbow is low then you need to let the ball drop before playing it. If the elbow is high then this will allow for fast movement from the shoulder (Fig. 45). It is important, because of the speed of movement, that the arm action is played in a circular motion and not a stop, start action. From the ready position the stroke is played with a circular motion back to the ready position. Move from the ready position to a side stance. Your stance should be fairly wide to take the strength of the stroke. Extra power is produced by turning the body and shoulders from the trunk upwards and the ball is hit with full power. Complete the circular motion of the stroke going back to the ready position (Fig. 46).

Backhand drive

The backhand drive like the forehand is a power stroke, but many players find that the forehand is more powerful than the backhand. This is mainly due to the stance. The forehand can be played from a side stance and the power can be transferred more easily; for the backhand the stance is square with the power of the stroke being played from the elbow and the wrist, in contrast to the forehand where the power is from the shoulder (Fig. 47). One of the problems often found when playing a power stroke from a square stance is that you may only have a small preparation to your stroke. If this happens, there tends to be a long follow-through – remember what was said earlier – the preparation is the important part of the stroke because once contact has been made with the ball nothing can add to the power imparted at contact. So save your energy on the follow-through, so that movement to the ready stance can be fractionally quicker. It is important to have a strong backhand as it is the backhand that opponents tend to attack, especially with their forehand, so when practising it is essential to have plenty of practice with backhand against forehand.

Smash (kill)

The smash should be mastered by all players. If you cannot smash the ball you will find point winning very difficult. The smash is played mainly with the forehand and is similar to that of the forehand drive but the power applied is greater. Tactically, a player should work all ploys around the smash and it should be used at the earliest opportune moment, by taking the poor chance or weak return and making it into a winner. When playing the smash, you should always be positioned so that you move to the ball and do not wait for the ball to come to you, as this will only result in a weak return. There are two variations to the smash: the compact smash and the dynamic smash.

Compact smash

This smash would be played over or at the end of the table, with a powerful compact movement. The basic requirement for the smash is to be relaxed as it is impossible to smash the ball if you are tense. Secondly, contact with the ball should be made just below shoulder level – this is where most power can be produced. Some coaches advocate smashing the ball at the peak of the bounce, but as some returns will be very high, this timing would not be correct. Some players try to make the smash seem more spectacular than it is – they play the smash whilst in mid-air. This is not really recommended on two counts:

1   Although you need to be mobile when playing this stroke, a firm base is also needed so that weight may be transferred efficiently. This cannot be done in mid-air.
2   This is a point of prime importance: when you have smashed the ball, you should always anticipate a return ball from your opponent. All he needs to do is to put his racquet in the way of the ball and it could rebound back, leaving you looking not so spectacular.

59

In the compact smash, the free and the playing arms are at 160 degrees. You should play from a side stance with one powerful movement. At completion of the stroke the stance is square; the arm is below head height in anticipation of any return (Fig. 48).

Dynamic smash
The dynamic smash is the same in principle as the compact smash but it is usually played away from the table. The base of the player is much wider as the movement in general is greater. Being away from the table allows more organisational time to play the stroke, and more time to recover into the ready position. Meet the ball when the stance is almost square. Because of the power of the stroke the back leg will come forward and the stance will become square to the side of the table (Fig. 49).

Fig. 47 Backhand drive

Fig. 48 Compact smash

Fig. 49A

Fig. 49B

Fig. 49C

Fig. 49D

Fig. 49E

Fig. 49 Dynamic smash

Practices for drive style
Phase 1

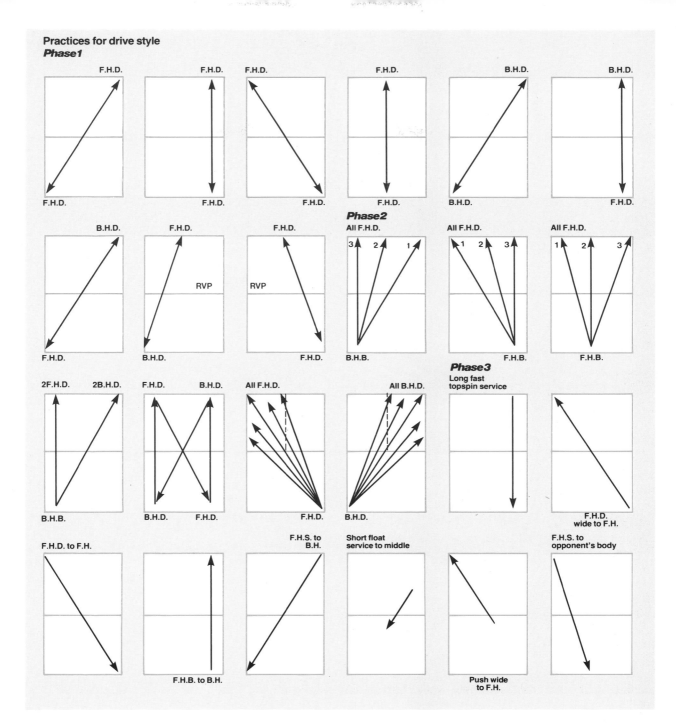

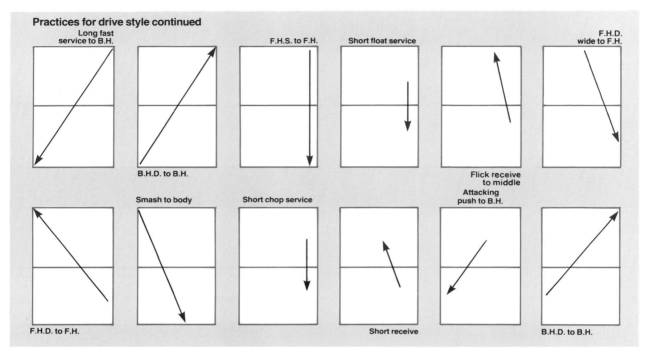

Practices for drive style continued

Long fast service to B.H. / B.H.D. to B.H. / F.H.S. to F.H. / Short float service / F.H.D. wide to F.H.

Smash to body / Short chop service / Flick receive to middle / Attacking push to B.H.

F.H.D. to F.H. / Short receive / B.H.D. to B.H.

Practice for the drive game, all styles of player

Phase 1

Practice for: stability play, grooving strokes, control over movements, control over ball, touch play.

Stability play, grooving strokes, control over movements apply to these practices as they did to previous ones. Players of all styles should practise driving the ball and blocking, as these strokes will be used at some stage in a game. The player who is practising the block should apply the correct amount of touch to the ball. When driving, vary the speeds; slow, medium and fast should be practised.

Phase 2

Practice for: footwork and varying timing.

Practise first regular footwork and then move on to irregular. With this type of game, running footwork will be used on some of the speed practices. Vary the timing between peak of bounce and early during your practice. Avoid using late timing when driving as you cannot play a power stroke on a late timing.

Phase 3

Practice for: point winning ploys.

The drive style player likes to win the point very quickly so the third and fifth; fourth and sixth ball attack will be used quite a lot by such players. You should also be on the offensive as much as possible with strokes such as the push and block. These should be attacking strokes. You need to take the poor chance and make it into a winner.

Abbreviations for drive style practices

F.H.D.	Forehand drive
B.H.D.	Backhand drive
F.H.B.	Forehand block
B.H.B.	Backhand block
F.H.S.	Forehand smash
R.V.P.	Reverse practice

Chapter 8 The use and effects of the combination racquet

The combination racquet is mainly used by backspin players and was first successful when used with anti-loop rubber on one side and a different type of rubber on the other. Later the long pimple rubber was introduced to the combination racquet to much greater effect. Because of this, combination racquets are widely and effectively used. The main advantage of long pimple rubber is that it is easy to counteract a hard drive or heavy spin and even a smash can be effectively returned. With this racquet, even with identical strokes and power, the amount and type of spin can vary widely.

The material of the blade (type of wood)

In the section on racquets I said that there were varying types of wood that could be used in the make-up of the racquet. The racquet blade most commonly used with long pimple rubber is a defensive type that will slow up the ball. But effects can be lost in playing with a defensive blade. One of the characteristics of the long pimple rubber is that against a slow ball it is ineffective and, if the long pimples are used for the return, a great amount of force is needed for that return. But if an all-round or offensive blade is used, then this will make the return more effective. The point then to consider when returning the ball with the inverted side of the racquet is – do you have control over the return?

Surface of the racquet (type of sponge and rubber)

	Side 1	Side 2
a)	Inverted sponge & rubber	Long pimple rubber only
b)	Inverted sponge & rubber	Long pimple rubber & sponge
c)	Inverted sponge & rubber	Anti-loop rubber
d)	Inverted sponge & rubber	Normal pimple rubber & sponge

The long pimples are made from soft rubber with the length of the pimples between 1.5mm and 1.7mm. The normal pimples are approximately 1mm long and these are made from harder rubber. The sponge backings are of various thicknesses and properties, thus giving varying characteristics to the rubber. The anti-loop rubber is made from very soft rubbers. Racquets made up of the rubbers of a), b) and c) would mainly be used by backspin players, and the d) combination would be more for the drive or topspin player. For the drive or topspin player it would be usual for the inverted side of the racquet to be used on the forehand and the normal pimples on the backhand. But in using combination racquet a), b) or c) you can confuse your opponent by playing both backhand and forehand with either side of the racquet (this is called *twiddling*). A player will play one stroke with the long pimples and then twiddle, spinning the racquet round so that the next return will be from the inverted side of the racquet. An experienced player may twiddle the racquet round up to four times before playing a stroke.

The use of long pimpled rubber can produce a variation of spin, from a ball with no spin (float) to a highly spun backspin ball. This will depend to some extent upon the type of ball received from the opponent. The combination racquet should be used so that you can use the long pimpled rubber to the best advantage. It is not an easy task to handle two variations in the rubber when each has a different characteristic and feeling when contacting the ball and it requires a great deal of practice to become competent. Using both sides of the racquet will give more possibilities and variations than using the one type of rubber on one side of the racquet for forehand strokes and the other side for backhand strokes. For example, if a player only uses long pimple on the forehand side and inverted on the backhand side, the opponent will soon know which side of the racquet has been used and will be able to make the appropriate return.

One point to remember when playing with a combination is to twiddle the racquet so that your opponent cannot see which side of the racquet has been used. This may be done in several ways. The first would be to play the ball on a late timing so that the ball will be below the level of the table. You could

twiddle so that your opponent would not be able to see which side of the racquet was used. The disadvantage with this is that the ball played on a late timing will have lost a great deal of its spin or speed. The second way, and this could be used when playing over the table, is, before playing the stroke, spin the racquet round by twiddling two or three times before making contact with the ball, or show one side of the racquet and go to play the stroke, then at the last moment twiddle the racquet round playing the ball with the alternative side. When serving many players hide the racquet below the table so that the opponent cannot see which side of the racquet has been used. The action of the service then needs to be exceptionally fast so that the opponent cannot see which side of the racquet is being used. With the racquet below the table, weigh up your opponent; with the racquet still below the table return your attention to the ball (Fig. 50). In Fig. 51 Huang Liang (China) shows an alternative method by holding the racquet horizontal.

Fig. 50 Weighing up your opponent

A show of aggression by Stellan Bengtsson

Fig. 51 Huang Liang (China)

Summary

The main advantage of long pimple rubber is that it is easy to counteract a hard hit, drive or heavy spin. Long pimple rubber possesses the characteristic of being able to return heavy backspin against a smash, loop or power drive. It is easy to block and float a ball. Deception, especially when serving, can be achieved; with an exaggerated swing it may look as if a large amount of spin is being imparted to the ball, but the service could be a ball with very little spin, thus confusing your opponent.

The disadvantages are that with long pimples it is not as easy to control the ball as it is with other types of rubbers. When the opponent returns a slow ball it is difficult to chop it. It is also difficult to hit hard and achieve speed when playing a stroke. The most effective way to play with a combination racquet is to make use of its advantages and minimise its disadvantages.

Expedite

All backspin players should be familiar with the *Expedite System,* as it is inevitable that at some stage in competition it will be introduced. It is advisable to practise playing expedite points.

If a game is unfinished after 15 minutes of play, the game is interrupted and the rest of that game, and the remaining games of the match, are played under the Expedite System. This means that if the service and 12 good returns of the serving player or pair are each followed by a good return by the receiving player or pair, the server loses a point. If the ball is in play when the game is interrupted, play is restarted with service by the player who served in the rally that was interrupted. If the ball is not in play when the game is interrupted, play is restarted with service by the player who received in the preceding rally.

The Expedite System may be introduced at any earlier time, from the beginning of the match up to the end of 15 minutes of play in any game, at the request of both players or pairs.

Chapter 9 **Variations in stroke play**

You should develop the ability to vary your strokes so that your opponent will find it hard to identify the spin, the speed and the direction of the ball. If you do not vary your returns your opponent will be able to anticipate very easily.

All strokes start with a preparatory movement before contact with the ball and if there is no váriation or deception in this movement the opposition will have no difficulty in identifying the stroke and the type of spin during the anticipation period.

By being able to vary strokes it will help you tactically to outplay your opponent by delaying his decision making and forcing him into an error. If you have no variation your opponent is at an advantage in that he has more time in which to take the necessary action. One of the ways to deny this advantage to your opponent is to have the minimal amount of preparation movement. This is particularly successful when serving. You can also vary the stroke by using a variety of racquet angles, thus using different contact points on the ball. If successful, you will have played the ball before your opponent can detect the type of return he is about to receive and before he can decide on a course of action. In reducing your preparation time you are also reducing your opponent's anticipation period. This increases the probability that your opponent will make a mistake.

All strokes should be efficient and effective and played with variation and deception – they should be developed with the minimum amount of time and energy. When putting this theory into practice, the following points need to be taken into consideration.

Many players and coaches are under the impression that practice makes perfect, but this is not true. For a player to improve in his execution of any skilled action, practices have to be set with a specific purpose in mind and players should know the goal at which they are aiming. In many practice programmes a player needs to groove his stroke so that it may be played automatically. Practice programmes often isolate skills, and it should be remembered that

a player needs to be able to read a situation. It is not enough just to practise strokes; players must also develop the skill of reading and the ability to play the appropriate shot.

If you are practising the backhand block with an opponent practising the forehand loop each player is using one type of stroke, so each player's return is predictable. Each knows the type of return and the type of spin on the ball, therefore there are no decisions to be made. This type of practice is good for grooving the stroke, for control, consistency and accuracy.

Although grooving strokes is essential, the danger with this type of practice is that the player knows beforehand what type of return he will receive and, during practice, responses become highly automatic. A player can become highly conditioned to that practice due to receiving the same stimulus at regular intervals, and this discourages adaptability. In this type of practice reaction time becomes shorter (it could be reduced to near zero) but when the practice is transferred to a match, the player's reaction time can become much longer due to the fact that during practice he has not learned to cope with the natural variation in an opponent's game.

Another type of practice is for one player to practise a backhand block and a forehand hit. The opponent is forehand hitting to three positions on the table. The opponent again is using one type of stroke only but playing the ball to three different positions. This type of practice is good for control consistency, rhythmic movement, footwork and balance, but here again the type of return and the direction of the ball is known in advance.

A third type of practice has one player using the backhand block or forehand hit, depending upon where the return is going but the ball must be returned to the opponent's forehand corner. The opponent is playing either a forehand loop or hit and the ball can be played anywhere on the player's side of the table. This type of practice has the same effect as the previous one but also introduces the element of anticipation. The type of stroke, spin and the direction of the ball all have to be anticipated. Developing this skill is just as important as perfecting strokes.

It is essential, while developing basic skills, that players are introduced to practice that is unpredictable. This type of practice is the nearest to match conditions that can be achieved through practices. The only element missing will be match stress, which no practice can produce.

Underlying factors in stroke play

One of the differences between a successful player and an average player lies in the ability to anticipate where the ball is going to be played, the amount of spin, the flight and the speed of the ball. The art of anticipation or cue recognition is to be organised to play your strokes effectively and efficiently. In other words, you need to be in the right place at the right time. This can be done by means of having the ability to anticipate and judge the intended action of your opponent.

How can a player develop and improve his anticipation? This is a difficult question. One way to improve anticipation is through competitive experience; another is through intelligent practice. It is a waste of time to organise practices where no anticipation is required.

First of all there are certain important factors to look for and to make decisions on during a rally. A common phrase used by both coaches and players is 'keep your eye on the ball'. This is true up to a point, but if a player keeps his eye on the ball all the time he will miss other important cues: the position of the opponent; the way the opponent is shaping up to play the next stroke. You need only keep your eye on the ball from the time that your opponent has made contact with the ball to the time that you make contact with the ball yourself. This is a basic principle that needs to be applied when playing a stroke. If you continue to watch the ball after playing your stroke, this will deprive you of information that is required to anticipate the playing of the next stroke. So, as well as keeping your eye on the ball, you must be alert to information transmitted by your opponent.

Information processing and cue recognition

Before you can play a stroke with confidence, you need to go through several processes and sequences to acquire the relevant information.

You must take in information from:
1   Your opponent's position
2   The way your opponent is shaping up

You must try to detect:
1   The type of stroke used
2   The direction of the ball
3   The spin and speed (flight) of the ball

You must decide:
1   Where to play the ball
2   Which stroke to use

All this information has to be processed within a fraction of a second, so if your attention is concentrated on the ball during this time then you are neglecting more important information. This should not only apply to competition, but also when practising. Many of the decisions are made subconsciously. In simple terms, the process is one of *Input, Decision making* and *Output.*

Input

Input is the information, based on the player's perceptions, which is relayed to the brain.

Decision making

The player then needs to decide on a course of action. This decision will only be successful if all relevant information has been perceived and the opponent's intentions accurately assessed.

Output

Output is the player's muscular response to the process of analysis and decision making.

In table tennis terms this is shown in Fig. 52. All rallies should be thought of as a chain of sequential actions repeated for as long as a rally lasts, whether that is for three strokes or for twenty-three.

Guo Yuehua shows he can attack even with a backhand block

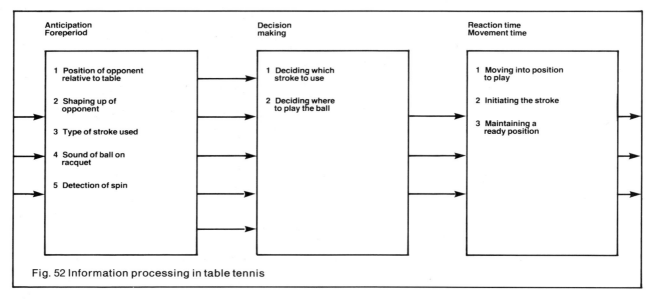

Fig. 52 Information processing in table tennis

Foreperiod (Anticipation)

This is the time interval between your return and the presentation of your opponent's stroke. It is important during the foreperiod that you anticipate the results of your own return and that you react to the expected stimulus as quickly as possible. If you use a weak chop return and it only lands in the middle of the table, your opponent's return stroke could be either a drop shot or a smash – you need to anticipate both types of return. Out of these points a good player will pick out very early in 'the display' the important factors and will act upon them. When reacting to a display there are three phases:

Input time

This is the time that it takes to absorb the signals:

1 Sound; you may hear the amount of spin given to the ball.
2 Sight; if your opponent is using a combination racquet you may see which side is being used. You may also perceive your opponent's actions and the bounce of the ball as it hits the table and is coming towards you.

Decision time

This is the time in which a player decides how to deal with the information received. It is essential to make the correct decision. All the hours of practice spent on grooving strokes can be wasted just because the wrong decision is taken.

Reaction time

This is the time it takes to initiate the response by the muscles. There is also *movement time* – this is the duration of the response.

Movement time (or organisational time)

This is the time taken to move into position and to become organised to play the relevant stroke. It is important to distinguish reaction time from movement time. A player could have a fast reaction time but be retarded by a slow movement time, caused by:

1 Poor balance and footwork (stance too wide)
2 Length of stroke used (preparation too long)
3 Slow joint movement due to lack of flexibility and mobility
4 Not using the correct joints

Chapter 10 Service technique

Just as it is necessary to be an individual in your style and technique, it is equally important to create an individual style of service. Many players regard service as a means of introducing the ball into play – this is wrong. The service is your first chance of winning a point. If you do not win the point on service, then you must attack the ball at the first opportune moment.

Principles of service technique

1 The first bounce: where you place the ball on your side of the table is of the utmost importance. If you want to play a short service the ball needs to be played near the net on your side of the table. If the service is to be long, then the first bounce needs to be around 20cm from the end line of the table (Fig. 53).

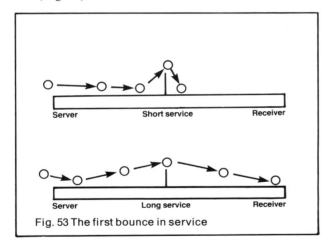

Fig. 53 The first bounce in service

2 The throw-up: the ball must be thrown up from the palm of the free hand; there is no defined height to which the ball must travel, but it must leave the palm of the hand. Vary the height to which you throw the ball from a high throw service, like that made popular by the Chinese, to a low throw where the ball just rises from the palm of the hand. The ball should be played on its descent (the law states) and it is this part which is of importance. The height at which the ball is struck, in relationship to the place on your side of the table, will have a great bearing upon the trajectory of the service (Fig. 54).

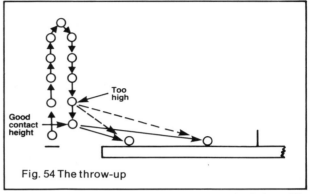

Fig. 54 The throw-up

The combination of these two principles will, to a great extent, determine the success of the service.

3 The type of spin: this will affect the height of the ball as it lands on your side of the table (Fig. 55).

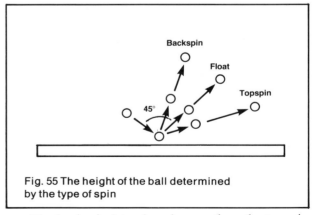

Fig. 55 The height of the ball determined by the type of spin

The backspin 'stands up' more than the topspin so that a short backspin service needs to be placed closer to the net so that it will clear it.

4 Source of power: when serving, the body should be used to help impart power to the serve. The

73

main source of the power will come from the movements of the elbow and wrist (the two fastest moving joints).

Service tactics

1 Use deception: you may thereby force an error from your opponent
2 Serve with the intention of creating an attacking opportunity
3 Keep the receiver from initiating an attack on your service

How can these three tactical principles be achieved? The first answer is very simple: spend a lot of time practising different types of service; develop a number of variations to each service. A successful combination of variety and deception will win most points. It may force your opponent to make a mistake or allow you to win the point by initiating a third ball attack.

The object is to vary your service but to use the same motions. You can vary the amount of spin and speed applied to the ball and make use of different contact points. You will deceive successfully if you can play one type of service and at the same time make it look like another. You could use the motion for a heavy chop serve and produce a service with no spin (float) thus forcing your opponent into an error. This will probably result in a high return which you can smash or a return off the end of the table. This idea could be reversed and a service which appears to be 'no spin' could in fact be chopped. Again your opponent may be forced to drive the ball into the net.

If your opponent is good at receiving service, it may be advisable to use a few short services in every five. This is where deception is really important. With a normal short service, your opponent could play a short return back keeping you on the defensive, but if you can add deception, your opponent will be more likely to make an error so that you can maintain your attack.

The trick of deception is to be able to alter the angle of the racquet on impact with the ball. If you play a stroke on a downwards movement you will impart backspin; if you play upward topspin and across the ball sidespin in a forward motion there will be no spin. If the ball is brushed lightly spin is produced, if contact is hard the ball will have no spin. If you hit the ball with a forward motion there will be less spin imparted (Fig. 56).

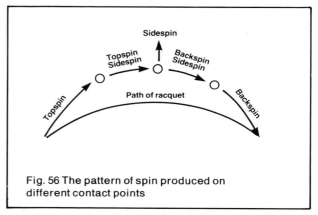

Fig. 56 The pattern of spin produced on different contact points

Fig. 57 Surbek (Yug.) showing a sidespin service

Pak Yung-Sun shows the use of the body when serving

In Fig. 57 Surbek serves a sidespin service with the racquet angle vertical. The racquet movement will be sideways to create sidespin, not speed.

From all these probabilities, with the addition of dexterity, you can contrive many deceptive services.

Principles of deception

1   Use the same motion for a number of services
2   Vary your wrist movement and angle on impact with the ball
3   Vary the touch when playing the ball
4   Vary the racquet angle on impact, and this in turn will vary the contact point on the ball
5   Use the same motion after impact with the ball when moving into the ready stance, thus disguising the type of spin on the ball

Short service

The short service is popular with the topspin player. If the service is very short with a large amount of spin on the ball, then your opponent will not be able to attack it. This service will be played from the backhand corner of the table, usually short on your opponent's forehand or short to middle on the forehand, as these are usually the susceptible positions. Two of the main principles to remember when serving short: a) there is no forward motion when the ball bounces on your opponent's side of the table; b) the ball is played close to the net on your side of the table.

Long service

This type of service is favoured by the drive players who like their opponents to play the ball hard to them so that they may attack the ball, or by the backspin player who likes his opponent to play the ball hard so that it can be chopped and kept long.

Tactically it may be found that if the game is very close, you may surprise your opponent, after mainly using short services, by serving long – your opponent will then be forced into an error and may set up an easy ball. Earlier I said that the height of the contact on the ball determines the height that the ball bounces on both sides of the table – drive players will in the main serve low, but they can occasionally use a higher contact point giving a high service which is normally played back relatively high; this is anticipated and smashed.

High throw service

The high throw service was first introduced by the Chinese and is very popular in today's game. If the ball is thrown high it will descend at greater speed and when the racquet makes contact a greater effect will be produced. The ball will gain maximum speed if it is thrown up to a height of around 10 metres – the speed of the ball on descent is about 30 km per hour. When using the high throw service:

1   Make use of the acceleration on the ball created from the descent
2   By throwing the ball high, draw your opponent's attention to the ball and not to the angle of the racquet
3   Your opponent's reaction time is delayed by the high throw
4   You can produce maximum amount of spin on the ball from a high service

The high throw service can be played by the backhand or forehand, but the forehand service is the one that is the most favoured as more power can be applied. It is usually played from the backhand corner of the table, mainly from a side stance position. This type of service follows the same principles as the low throw service but you need to be positioned a little farther away from the table. When you throw the ball up it needs to be thrown a little forward; latitude of 45 degrees is allowed in the laws. As the ball is thrown high it gives more organisational time so that you may use your trunk by twisting the body and arm to produce maximum power to the service. In Fig. 58 Orlowski (CZE) shows the high service with the twist from the trunk for additional power and with the free arm giving balance.

Fig. 58 Orlowski (CZE) shows the high service

Fig. 59 Thorsell (Sweden) shows a variation

All these principles result in greater speed and a stronger spin service. It is important that the wrist and arm should be relaxed before playing the ball and at the last moment of impact you should apply all the power of the wrist, arm and body quickly to the ball. In Fig. 59 Thorsell (Sweden) serves with the racquet held high, but the ball will be struck low giving fast movement from the shoulder, elbow and especially the wrist.

The ball should be played so that it is about 20 cm above table height before impact and about 20 cm from the end line so that it will not lose spin or speed. If the bounce is half-way down the table it will lose its effect.

77

Sidespin service

Sidespin service is also widely used in today's game. The service can be long or short, making the ball break in various directions, depending upon the type and degree of sidespin with the possible addition of either topspin or backspin. A variety of sidespin services must be acquired. The sidespin service changes direction as it lands on your opponent's side of the table. It is of prime importance to have a clear idea of the amount and type of spin and its effect from the service, especially when playing the third ball.

If the emphasis is mainly upon sidespin then the racquet should be vertical and the contact point on the ball should be played horizontally across the ball so that there is no forward movement to the ball (Fig. 57). The same principles apply for a normal short service. There are players who when playing a sidespin service use a downward and upward movement; this way they have three alternative services (Fig. 56):

1   Sidespin with backspin

2   Mainly sidespin

3   Sidespin and topspin

These are in the main short services.

If you use a long sidespin service, then the switch service is one that will often catch your opponent out. The same principles are used as for the high throw service, but on contact with the ball the angle of the racquet is changed, producing a different contact point (Fig. 60). This results in a long diagonal service into your opponent's backhand or straight down the forehand, giving the ball enough sidespin so that it breaks away from your opponent. You must decide upon the type of service you are going to play and also whether the emphasis is to be on spin or speed. If the racquet is played with a forward motion, this will tend to make it a speed ball rather than a spin ball. Practise increasing the speed of the racquet swing to make it as fast as possible. Although the racquet is moving quickly, the speed of the ball should be

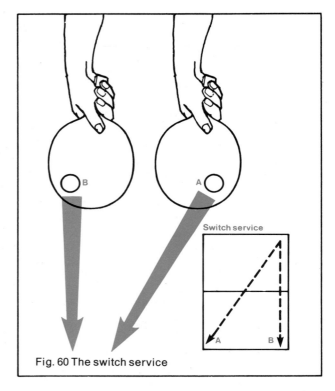

Fig. 60 The switch service

relatively slow, and the energy put into the motion of the racquet must be converted into spin and not speed. It is important to check the placement of the ball on your side of the table – if it is too near to the end line of the table it becomes more of a speed ball than a spin ball as you will need to play the ball with greater forward motion to ensure that it will go over the net.

There are two final points that I would like to make on service:

a)   You must master a wide variety of services and you must be able to play and co-ordinate them with an attack on the third ball (see Chapter 11).

b)   You will be serving for about half of the game – it is up to you to try to take the initiative.

Isvan Jonyer, caught wide on the forehand, maintains balance

Chapter 11 **Receive of service**

Just as it is the server who has the first opportunity to win the point, if he fails to achieve this it then becomes the receiver's opportunity. A player who can dominate play from his receive can dominate the game. If you have poor receiving technique this will make winning a difficult task. We should first divide the receive into two categories:

1   Attack receive
2   Control receive

A player should mainly attack the service and only use a control receive when a tight serve is played. The latter will mainly be from a short service.

When receiving service you should:

1   Take up the ready position to a specific line of play. This really refers to topspin and drive players who take up the ready stance on the backhand side of the table, and this should be adjusted if the server adjusts the position from where he is to serve.

2   Watch closely the shaping up of the server and as he starts moving, so should the receiver. It takes time to become mobile and if the receiver only starts to move when the server has played the ball it could be on his side of the table before he becomes fully mobile. All that is needed is that the feet should be moving in the ready stance. Take care not to move too much, as this could affect your balance. If you move your weight onto the left foot, the server might see this and serve fast to the right side of your body – the weight should be kept evenly balanced.

3   Watch for the height of contact on the ball and also the angle of the racquet, especially on contact with the ball. Watch the movement of the wrist and elbow looking for deceptive movement, especially if the server has made contact with the ball.

4   Anticipate from the actions of your opponent, and move efficiently into position to play your stroke. Before playing your stroke double check the nature of the service by closely watching the ball bounce, both on the server's side of the table and on your own side. Many players look for the trade mark on the ball to detect which way the ball is spinning – this requires a great deal of visual acuity – with practice it can be done.

Just as the server has to vary the service, so too has the receiver to vary the returns to effective parts of the table. You need a full understanding of how to attack or control effectively the receive of service and you must also appreciate the full implications and purpose of the receive of service.

What is the most effective way of receiving the service? It is for the receiver to take the advantage as quickly as possible. If playing a control receive you should place the ball so that the return from the server (the third ball) cannot be attacked, or alternatively play the receive out of the opponent's reach – an effective place is usually wide to the opponent's forehand. If you use a control receive then you should attempt to attack the fourth ball.

Playing against a short service

The effective way to return a short service is to attack it unless it is tight. A short service should bounce twice on the receiver's side of the table, so the most effective way of dealing with this is to use an attacking push stroke.

Remember the earlier advice about using the outside of the racquet for this stroke. A good attacking push is quite effective if played to the right hand side of your opponent's body. Another way is to use the flick – this will only be used against a short ball. There are two ways that this can be done against a short service to the forehand. One is to go close to the table placing the right foot well under the table and then playing the flick (Fig. 61). The problem with this is that the player is restricted in the body area and only the arm joints such as the elbow and wrist are used. The alternative is to go into the table with the left foot – this allows use of the body and the arm, including the shoulder (Fig. 62).

Fig. 61 Attacking the short service

Fig. 62 An alternative attack

When playing against a short service which cannot be attacked, the control return should be played back short so that the server cannot attack the return. A word of warning though: if the third ball is returned short you should try to open out with an attack on the fourth ball by playing the ball long to an effective position.

Playing against a long service

When receiving a long or a medium length service, you must judge the speed and spin, the direction of the ball and in particular the length of the ball. You must also judge how high the ball will be when it reaches the edge of the table so that the appropriate attacking stroke can be applied to return. Try to avoid negative blocking and push returns and always try to attack.

The backspin player should not always receive by using a chop return but should acquire a wide range of receives – this will prevent the server taking the advantage from the backspin player's stereotype return. Instead of using a chop return you should use a hard drive if a fast service is delivered. The varied returns will make it difficult for the server to play positively on the third ball.

Third and fifth ball attack

The service is the first ball, the receive the second, the return to the server is the third, then follow the fourth, fifth, sixth and so on.

The service and the third and fifth ball attack principle was first introduced by the Chinese and is considered one of the most important factors in point winning in today's game. It is now used world-wide by all styles of player, in particular the drive and top-spin players whose use of their repertoire of ploys is their main way of point winning. It is also equally important for the backspin style player to incorporate the third ball attack in his strategy. The use of the third and fifth ball attack is a positive ploy and the player should be aware of the tactical objectives and be aware of the success and failure rate during a game.

After practising specific strokes it is necessary to combine them into specific tactical ploys by making up third and fifth ball attacks.

Winning a point

There are three ways to win a point:

1   By forcing the ball past your opponent
2   By forcing your opponent into an error
3   By an unforced error from your opponent

Third ball attack

There are two main requirements for a successful third ball attack. The first is for a technically strong service. A player will mainly use a long service if employing the third ball attack, as a long return is required. If this ploy is used with a short service you will need to be deceptive to lead your opponent into making a high return; the third ball can then be smashed. The second requirement is for a speed ball (one that has been driven or smashed). This has the highest ratio of success in point winning, so the third ball needs to be a speed ball. Therefore, to be successful with the third ball attack, you need to combine good service with a strong drive or smash on the third ball. Use the practice tables on page 83.

Fifth ball attack

The fifth ball attack has the same requirements as the third ball attack – good service technique followed up by a speed ball. But this time the third ball, although the stroke is strong, is usually a topspin stroke which will force the opponent into a weak return, then on the fifth ball a strong drive or smash can be used to win the point. Use the practice tables on page 83.

Remember, however, that you will not always achieve your objectives and if you fail to win the point on the third ball, then you must try to succeed on the fifth. If this again fails, it is important to maintain the offensive by attacking the seventh ball and so on.

Third ball attack

Row 1:
1 — Long service
2 — B.H.D.
3 — F.H.S.
1 — Long service
2 — B.H.B.
3 — F.H.S.

Row 2:
1 — Long service
2 — F.H.D.
3 — F.H.S.
1 — Long service
2 — F.H.B.
3 — F.H.S.

Fifth ball attack

Short B.H. sidespin with backspin service

1
2 — F.H.P.
3 — F.H.S.L.
4 — F.H.B.
5 — F.H.S.

Short B.H. float service

1
2 — Short return to middle
3 — Long attacking push wide to B.H.
4 — Long B.H.P.
5 — F.H.S.

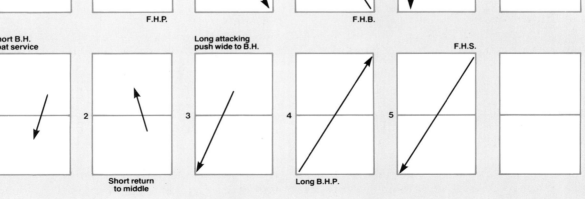

83

Fourth ball attack

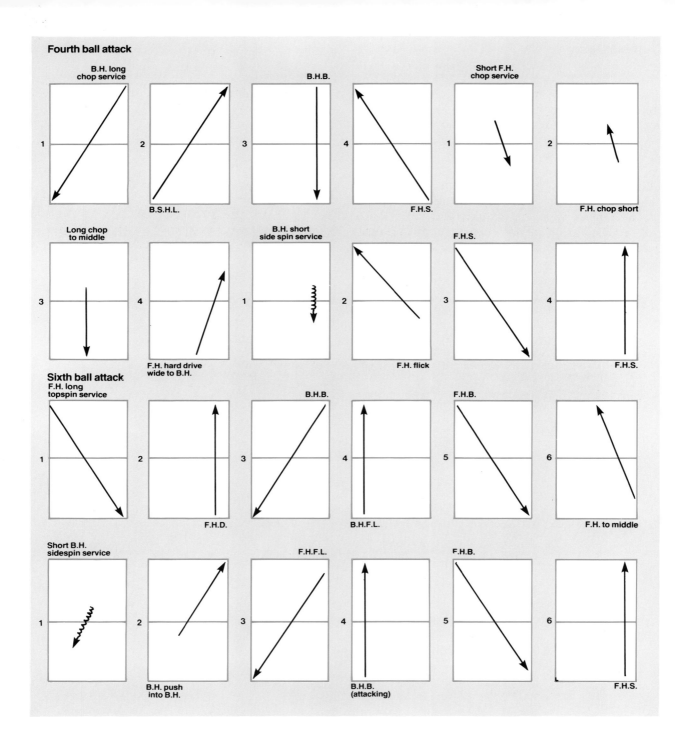

B.H. long chop service

1 — B.S.H.L.

2 — B.S.H.L.

B.H.B.

3

4 — F.H.S.

Short F.H. chop service

1

2 — F.H. chop short

Long chop to middle

3

4 — F.H. hard drive wide to B.H.

B.H. short side spin service

1

2 — F.H. flick

F.H.S.

3

4 — F.H.S.

Sixth ball attack

F.H. long topspin service

1

2 — F.H.D.

B.H.B.

3

4 — B.H.F.L.

F.H.B.

5

6 — F.H. to middle

Short B.H. sidespin service

1

2 — B.H. push into B.H.

F.H.F.L.

3

4 — B.H.B. (attacking)

F.H.B.

5

6 — F.H.S.

Fourth and sixth ball attack

Just as there is the third and fifth ball attack for the server, there is also the fourth and sixth for the receiver. Although the player who is serving has the first advantage, it is up to the receiver to take the initiative from the server. Like the server the receiver should have good technique and should attempt to be on the offensive, first of all by stopping a third ball attack from the opponent and then launching a fourth ball attack by the use of a strong ball. The same principle applies for the sixth ball attack. Use the practice tables on page 84.

Tactically, these ploys should be used throughout the game. When they are used in the first part of the game you should note the ones you are having success with and the ones that are not so successful. For it is in the latter part of a game, when the pressure is on, that you should launch your third and fifth or fourth and sixth attacks, using the ploys that won points in the earlier part of the game. It is a good idea to use this strategy if the score is 20 all, or if you are 20 – 18 down – you should try not to go on the defensive. If you go on the defensive and wait for your opponent to make the mistake then you may have to wait too long.

Abbreviations for third and fifth ball practices

F.H.S.	Forehand smash
F.H.D.	Forehand drive
B.H.D.	Backhand drive
F.H.B.	Forehand block
B.H.B.	Backhand block
F.H.P.	Forehand push
B.H.P.	Backhand push
F.H.S.L.	Forehand slow loop

Abbreviations for fourth and sixth ball practices

B.S.H.L.	Backhand slow high loop
F.H.B.	Forehand block
B.H.B.	Backhand block
F.H.S.	Forehand smash
F.H.D.	Forehand drive
F.H.F.L.	Forehand fast loop
B.H.F.L.	Backhand fast loop

Chapter 12 Training

Fitness training is a complex subject open to many theories. There is no one fitness training programme to meet all players' requirements – the topspin player will need a different training programme from the backspin player. You must consider the level of play at which you are competing and also your age. All these factors need to be taken into consideration before thinking about fitness training for table tennis.

Some people maintain that a player receives enough exercise while practising and competing – this is true for the 'once a week' player. However, for the aspiring player a fitness programme is essential.

Consider first of all the areas of fitness:

1 Endurance
2 Strength
3 Speed
4 Power
5 Flexibility

The first objectives should be to develop general fitness through a programme that includes Aerobic endurance, strength, speed and mobility. It is important to note at this point that it would be a waste of time to train by doing only one exercise per week. To develop general fitness you must include in your training programme exercises at least three times a week to achieve your objectives. This applies to all areas of exercise. The length of time for general fitness to develop is about three to four weeks if the exercises are done on a regular basis. Before doing any exercise it is essential to have a full body warm-up which should include flexibility and stretching exercises, as follows:

Warm-up exercises

1	Jogging and sprinting	2 minutes
2	Co-ordinated skipping	2 minutes
3	Jogging – alternating forwards, sideways and backwards (rhythmically)	2 minutes

Neck exercises

4	Neck circling	5 times each way
5	Neck stretch	5 times

Shoulders

6	Arm circling – forward and back	10 times
7	Arm pressing and flinging – elbows bent for 2 then fling arms out straight for 2	5 times
8	Arm circling with alternate rotation each way	10 times
9	Elbow circling forwards and backwards	10 times
10	As 9 but fast	10 times

Back and spine

11	Side bends – 2 left, 2 right	10 times
12	As 11 but introduce free arm overhead	10 times
13	As 11 but introduce both arms overhead	10 times
14	Legs wide astride, touch floor twice and overhead twice	5 times
15	As 14 but wider astride, touch floor with elbow	5 times
16	Trunk twist to left and right	10 times

Hip joints and hamstring

17	Sit in hurdling position a) Touch toes left and right	10 times
	b) Cross leg over outstretched leg, touch toes	10 times
18	Sitting, heels drawn in, shake knees	10 times
19	Crouch position leg stretching, keeping fingers on floor	10 times
20	Forward lunge	10 times
21	Side lunge	10 times
22	As 21 but alternate side	10 times

Ankle

23	Sitting, leg bent, hold one leg off floor with arm tucked behind knee, rotate foot inward and outward	10 times
24	Squatting, knees out, raise on toes and down	10 times

| 25 | Squatting, knees out, press down on outside of foot | 10 times |

Wrist

26	Rotate wrists forwards and backwards	10 times
27	Palms together press wrist down left and right	10 times
28	Rotate held wrists	10 times
29	Loose jogging – ease down	2 minutes

Endurance

Endurance is required in two areas:

1   To improve the cardio-vascular system (or Aerobic endurance)
2   To develop endurance in the areas of the arms and legs

A method of developing the cardio-vascular system (i.e. developing heart and lung efficiency) would be distance running, for example, a timed five kilometre run or the twelve minute run, measuring the distance covered. This is a popular way of increasing Aerobic endurance. If you cover more than three kilometres this would be excellent; if the distance is less than one and a half kilometres you will need to do a lot of work in this area as this is very poor. Local muscular endurance is required in the arms and legs – running will help the legs, but the main source of developing muscle endurance is with weight training or circuit training.

Strength

The strength that is required for table tennis is general strength to develop muscles and not the pure strength that is required to move heavy loads. A player needs general strength to develop power. Again, this can be achieved through weight training and circuit training. Weight training is not recommended for the young player (under the age of 12) and all such training should be carried out either under continued expert guidance or with initial expert planning and supervision.

Weight training programme

At 60 per cent of maximum, three times eight repetitions:

1   High pull up
2   Press behind neck
3   Two hand curl
4   Dumb-bell side bend
5   Bend forward rowing
6   Back squats
7   Power clean
8   Bench press
9   Straight arm pull over
10 Twisting sit up

Speed

There are two types of speed required, organisational speed and speed of movement. Again weight training can be used to improve speed. Shadow play with dumb-bells is another way, but sprinting is the main way of improving speed in the legs.

Exercises

Sprint 30 metres, 30 times or
Sprint for 5, 10, 15 seconds, 5 times

Shadow play

Shadow play is an effective way to improve your stroke play and to improve the speed of movement that you make by swinging your arm. The beauty of this type of training is that you do not necessarily need a table and you do not need a ball. It can be done in the privacy of your bedroom and it is better if it can be performed in front of a mirror so that you can observe the movements and analyse them. There are special weighted racquets for shadow play, but if you do not have a weighted racquet then a dumb-bell could be used.

Shadow play can help you to improve your technique. One of the objects in table tennis is to groove a stroke so that it becomes a reflex action. When you are developing a skill your attention is mainly upon the ball and not on your movement. By

87

using shadow play your attention can be devoted to your movement, and by analysing the movement observed in the mirror you will be helped to develop the movement required. You should see that your stance is correct, that your weight is transferred, that there is good co-ordinated movement from both upper and lower parts of the body and that the swing from the playing arm is correct. In particular see that it is a complete body movement and not just a swing from the arm. This should be done for about five minutes at varying speeds, then have a rest before repeating.

Shadow play can improve speed of movement. Follow the usual procedure, but instead of using your normal racquet, or no racquet at all, use a weighted racquet or a dumb-bell and instead of playing for five minutes play for one minute then rest for half a minute. You can do this five times depending upon the weight of the racquet or dumb-bell. Ensure that the weight is not too heavy and that the technical movements of the stroke are not affected in any way.

An alternative exercise would be for you to use a weighted racquet or dumb-bell for one minute and then switch to a very light racquet that has no rubber on it, which will make it lighter still. This will give you the effect of great speed of movement in your stroke.

You can also incorporate footwork into your shadow play routines. It would be best to do this at the table so that you cover approximately the same area that you will cover during a match, moving from side to side and in and out to the table, combining strokes and making up ploys such as third and fifth ball attack. The added advantage of this form of training is that you do not need a partner.

Power

Power is a combination of strength and speed and is mainly required in the legs. The form of training needed to improve power is bounding, which is a form of dynamic jumping.

Exercises

1	Standing broad jump	3 times
2	Hop, step, jump	3 times
3	2 hops, 2 steps, jump	3 times
4	2 hops, 2 steps, jump	3 times
5	2 hops, 2 steps, 2 jumps	3 times
6	5 spring jumps	3 times
7	4 hops and jumps	3 times

Flexibility

A player requires a full range of movement in all the relevant joints that are used when playing a stroke. If there is any tightness in the joints then this will retard the movements. Ways of improving flexibility are Yoga exercises or mobility exercises.

Training for competition

Training for competition needs to be well planned. Today, the competition at club level and also on the tournament circuit is overcrowded both at junior and senior level. The demands upon the players mean that they could be asked to compete on several occasions every week throughout the season. This is too demanding. No one can compete at this rate and remain in peak condition, especially not junior players. Time is needed to develop certain technical abilities and, if this time is not made available, improvements will not be made and poor techniques will become ingrained.

The season should be divided into various periods. This method, called *periodised training*, was first introduced by a Russian sports professor, L P Matrever, and it has been successfully adapted to table tennis. According to this method of training the year is divided into special periods during which a player would have specific aims in physical, technical, psychological and competitive areas.

Preparation period, Phase 1

During this period the player will work to develop all-round fitness, especially *endurance, strength, speed, power* and *flexibility*. During this period the player will also concentrate on technical development, such as developing strokes appertaining to the player's style of play.

Special training, Phase 2

This is training to perfect the player's individual skills and techniques and also to develop specific fitness. A drive player may require extra speed work or speed of arm movement, or a topspin player may need to increase strength in the legs.

Completion periods (training), Phase 3

Here technique is developed together with the practice of ploys, such as third and fifth ball attacks.

It is preferable for all training to be in a competitive situation and try-outs in small competitions.

Competition period, Phase 4

During this period the player should produce optimal performance in key competition that was planned at the beginning of the training period.

Transition period, Phase 5

In this part of the season there will be no competition and very little table tennis. On the physical side players participate in other sports, for example, squash, swimming, football, to maintain fitness.

Chapter 13 Competitions

A game is a battle

An old Chinese tactician once said, 'If you know yourself and your opponent fully before a battle, you will never lose the battle'. A game is a battle between two or more players. To succeed in this battle you must be well prepared for the various conditions and situations that you will meet. It is not always the best player who wins, but the one who is best prepared at the right time. You go into battle with the weapons prepared and learnt during training. You might be inferior in skill and technique but have superior fighting spirit and this will often allow you to succeed. The battle should commence before you go to the table. You should weigh up the enemy and anticipate the strategies that could be used against him. Your tactics should be backed up by the accuracy and skill developed during training. But you should have prepared more than one strategy for the battle, as the first may not work. If you show signs of tension the enemy can act on this and it could be your downfall.

Mistakes are inevitable during a battle and can be acceptable in the early part of a game only because you will have a chance to recover from the mistakes and still win. You need continually to assess the various stages of a battle. Win or lose, you should start the next battle without showing your feelings.

Preparing for battle

Your first consideration is how long will the battle last? Are you playing in a tournament over two days, or are you playing in a club match where you will only be playing two or three singles games in an evening? Is the competition the best of three or the best of five games? Will your physical and psychological preparation last over the given period and is your skill level good enough for you to win or achieve good results in the competition? If you think of international players at a World or European Championship, they have to be at their best for 10 days in succession if they are to come out as victors.

The next factors to consider are the playing conditions and equipment. One of the problems with table tennis is that there are no rigid stipulations for playing conditions. You might be confronted with a stone, wooden or linoleum floor. The type of floor will have a bearing upon the pace of the game. If it is a stone floor, the pace is usually fast and if it is a linoleum covered floor, it is usually slow. How high is the ceiling? If it is a low ceiling you can hear the ball much better than when the ceiling is high. If you practise in a venue with a low ceiling you have a cue in the sound of the ball played by your opponent and the sound of the ball as it bounces on your side of the table. This sound could be lost in a large sports hall. What will the lighting be – very bright or just adequate? Check the type of tables to be used and in particular the type of balls to be used. Try to arrange some practice on that type of table with that type of ball. Different makes of table give varying bounces. Will the ball be made of plastic or cellulose? Again, you will feel a difference in the bounce, the spin and in particular your touch play when playing services; the ball could vary from being very hard to very soft. All these factors will have a great bearing upon the results that you will achieve.

If you are preparing for competition, try to simulate the playing conditions and equipment you will meet and try to assess your opponent's game. Try also to practise at the time of day that you are going to play in competition. For example, whether you are going to play at 7.30 pm or 9.00 am will influence your performance. It is important if your match is at 9.00 am, that you are up at least two hours before you play. It is no use rolling out of bed and hoping to play well; it takes time for the biological workings of the body to become fully functional. This factor differs from person to person. I know very good competitors who cannot play well first thing in the morning. Take note of the times you play well and the times when you feel lethargic, so that you may be fully prepared for the battle in hand. Consider also the travelling time before a competition. No matter how you travel – by car, bus, or train, fatigue will occur. If you cannot arrive the night before the competition then you should try to arrive at the venue at least an hour before you have to play so that you can rest and acclimatise yourself to the conditions. Always try to practise on the table that you are going to play your match on and try to practise with a player who has a similar style to that of your opponent. If your opponent is a topspin player, it would be no use practising against chop. First practise consistency play, backhand and forehand, then move on to footwork practice. If your opponent knows you and you know that he will play into one particular part of the table, set the exercise first using regular then irregular practice to that area. Then move on to service and receive – again ask your practice partner to simulate the type of service you will encounter during the match. Finish the practice with third and fifth ball attacks as it is these ploys that can be real match winners.

You will have done a lot of preparation already for the competition, but about 20 minutes before playing is the time you should spend with last minute adjustments and the finalising of your preparations for the battle. You should spend this time away from the playing area, preferably somewhere quiet and away from any distractions and interruptions. During this period you will prepare yourself physically and psychologically. First, start with a light warm up. This warm up is different to the one that you would use during training and is much shorter, but it needs to be a full body warm up.

Warm up for match play
1 Light jog
2 Movement from side to side, also jumping up and down using varying movements from slow and sustained, to fast and dynamic
3 Mobility and stretching for arms and shoulders
4 Mobility and stretching for trunk
5 Mobility and stretching for hips
6 Mobility and stretching for legs, including feet
See that the whole of the body is fully warmed up

before you play. As you are doing your warm up exercises also do your mental preparation by thinking of the tactics and ploys you will use during the match. Always have an alternative plan in case the first does not work. Use shadow play simulating the strokes that you will use during the game. Shadow play should give you confidence in your stroke. Around 10 minutes before the match, go back into the playing area so that you can feel the atmosphere and also acclimatise your eyes to the light. Avoid talking to other players and keep calm – it will be this calmness that will help you through the game psychologically. If you are playing in a team game and your team mate is involved in a very close contest where the players and spectators are excited, try not to get involved, because if you become excited it could affect your performance, especially if your team mate loses. This is not bad team spirit, it is just common sense.

Tactics
Tactics is a very complex subject, as the opponents you will meet will all have various strengths and weaknesses to their individual styles of play. All tactics need to be related to two main factors:
1 Your own style of play and technical ability
2 Your opponent's style of play and technical ability
One of the most effective tactics during a game is that of changing the rhythm and speed of play. By deliberately varying the rhythm and speed it can effectively disrupt your opponent's rhythm and can also affect his timing. This is particularly effective if applied during a fast rally: to change the speed of play by a slow controlled return is a very effective ploy. But, if your opponent is matching you for speed and it is difficult for you to vary the speed of play, then you should change your tactics by reverting to spin. If you spin the ball effectively then your opponent will have to give a controlled return, enabling you to take the initiative by going on the offensive.

You will find that many players during a game will play safe and many of their returns will come off the end of the table. In your tactics, make full use of the table by using the angles so that the ball will go off the side lines of the table. Angling the ball can be one of the most effective ways of winning a point, and using this ploy is most effective especially if your opponent has poor footwork. Switch your opponent from side to side forcing him into making an error – this is very useful especially when playing your opponent wide to the forehand and then switching to his backhand. It is this type of ploy that has made the Chinese so effective with their fine service and their close to the table fast hitting, making full use of their acute angled hitting.

Into battle
From the outset it is essential that you take the initiative and strike the first blow. This means that you do not wait to see what your opponent is going to do. It should be you who dictates the course of the game. Always try to take the advantage by getting off to a good start. Remember the service is the first opportunity to win the point, so take the initiative and try to win your first five services. This can be worked out before you go to the table. By the same token, when your opponent serves and you are receiving, try to win at least three points from his service. If you can do this then you have taken the initiative and also gained a psychological advantage.

A game can swing from you having a good lead to you being in a losing position. Always be aware of the score line during a game; note where the points are being won and lost and with which tactics. Be particularly observant with regard to the winning and losing of points in succession. Do not play on regardless; take a breather by towelling down so that you may re-assess the situation and adjust your strategy to meet it.

Points are precious, so do not waste them, especially in the early part of a game. If the return from your opponent just clips the net and lands on your side of the table, do not leave it thinking that he has just won a lucky point. Make every effort to return the ball. This can be the difference between winning 21 to 19 and losing 19 to 21. This also applies to returns that clip the edge of the table. If things are not going too well for you during a match and you are well down, do not despair. Take a chance and do something different – you have nothing to lose. You can afford to take a chance.

Learn from a lost point
You should not ponder or worry when you lose a point. You cannot change the score line and if you worry you cannot give your 100 per cent concentration to the task in hand, but you can learn from a lost point. If your opponent is being effective with his service and you are having difficulty in reading the amount of spin on the ball, when your opponent serves a 'let service' do not just pick up the ball and give it back to him. Let the ball bounce on the table and look closely at the type and amount of spin on the ball. This also applies to stroke play, if you are playing against a backspin player and he is varying the spin. If you play a ball into the net, look closely at the amount of spin on it, so that you can use alternative measures to counter the spin. This also applies if the ball overshoots the table on your side. Let the ball bounce on the floor and look closely at it. *Learn from a lost point.*

Know your enemy
We have said that a game is a battle and your enemy for that duration is your opponent. It is always advantageous to know about the enemies that you are to meet in combat. You should know first of all their style of play, whether they are topspin, drive or backspin players. You should know their strong points just as well as you know their weak points. For example, where does their strength lie in their stroke play? If your opponent is a loop or drive type player he could be very strong from his backhand side of the table with his forehands and dictate the course of the game from that position. By the same token he could be weak if the ball is played wide to his forehand (left-handed players are usually weak in this position). Or, if your opponent is a backspin player, does he use

heavy chop and also have good variation in spin when playing strokes from the backhand? Also, if the ball is played to the forehand, does he only send a float return? All of these points need to be taken into consideration.

Note the movements of your opponent. Is he weak when moving from left to right or vice versa? Or, is he weak when moving in and out from the table? Backspin players are usually weak at this movement. Remember that when you are serving it is your first opportunity to win a point, so to know how your opponent receives your service will have a great bearing upon how successful you will be at winning points. It is important that early on in the game you find where your opponent is weak in receive of service, not only the position on the table but also the type – spin or float. If the scores are close in the latter part of the game then you will have to call upon the service to be effective. Service to and receive from your opponent are two of the most important factors to consider when looking for strength and weakness in an opponent, as it is these two points that have a great bearing upon the outcome and the course of a game.

Always be aware of the psychological state of your opponent during a game. The type of competition you are participating in will affect the mental state of your opponent. For example, if you are playing in a team competition your opponent might be selfish and only want to play for himself and his interest may be only in his own individual results; he will therefore not be a good team competitor. Or, your opponent may not be able to take the pressure of winning upon himself. If the score in the team match is three all and yours is the deciding match, then your opponent may be afraid of the situation and put up little or no resistance in the match. Or, on the other hand, he could be mentally strong in such situations and be a good fighter. If you are playing in a tournament and your opponent in the previous round has just had a good victory then psychologically he could be high and full of confidence; watch closely for this as he could also be over-confident. Note whether your opponent soon becomes despondent during a game when you use a particular service or stroke, or if the score line is not in his favour. Always observe these points and use them to your advantage.

Playing to the opponent's weakness

Use your knowledge and observations intelligently. If your opponent is weak in one particular place do not always play to the weak point. It is good strategy also to play to his strong points and then switch to his weak point. Your opponent will usually have more than one weak point so switch your attention by using the various tactics that you have devised. By using this type of strategy your opponent will not be able to settle down to play the type of game he wants to play. However, you must take care not to upset your own game by using these strategies. If you find that a particular service is effective and you are winning the point either on the service or the third ball, do not use it all the time as your opponent may find a way to handle it with an effective counter-stroke. Furthermore, you may need such a service in reserve if the game becomes close at the end.

Know yourself

Your prime aim when playing in a game is to win. If you are going to win then there is only one way and that is to *be positive in everything you do*. This not only applies to the competitive side of the game, but also to your training and practice. There are many attributes that make a champion. There are three main areas – *tactics, physical condition* and *psychological approach* and it is in these areas that you need to *know yourself*. A lot of hard work is needed to achieve your goal and this means, if you are to succeed, that you discipline yourself in every way; you must be determined and sure of your purpose. If, for example, endurance is the weak point in your physical condition and you are trying to rectify it, there is no point attempting a five kilometre run and after running three kilometres giving in to your tiredness. Pace yourself instead, or take a little rest and then complete the run.

93

When practising, do not always practise the things you can do well or like to do.

Table tennis usually requires a high level of skill from a player, but it is not always the ultimate factor. A player may be extremely talented with a high level of skill, but he might not have the psychological stability to stay calm in a tight competitive situation. This type of player usually crumbles and loses the battle. On the other hand a player's skill level may be only average, but his psychological application may be high and he can succeed in winning the battle. It is this combination of skill, physical and psychological factors which determines how successful a player will be in competition. It is up to you and your coach to develop to the full potential the areas where you are strong and also to strengthen your weak points.

Earlier in this section I said that the psychological factors were important especially in a competitive situation where tension and emotions really show. It is natural to be nervous before and at the beginning of a game. But it is not natural for you to have nervous tension. If you become psychologically tense you will also tense your muscles. This will affect your stroke play and you will be unable to play your strokes effectively. Try to keep calm and relaxed throughout the game. This can be achieved by relaxation exercises such as deep breathing – this can be effective during a game if you feel that your nerves are getting the better of you. You can improve your psychological side by relaxation exercises, but these will take a long time to develop and it is difficult for some people. For relax- ation, you should be in a quiet place, either sitting or lying down. Start relaxing from the feet and toes for around three seconds; do this three times then go on to the lower part of the legs, then the upper part of the legs and so on until you have completely relaxed the whole of the body. With your whole body now re- laxed, turn your mind to one subject, something you like such as a flower or a bird – if your mind wanders from the subject take it back immediately. This form of exercise should be done daily; it will take a long time to develop but it will be worthwhile.

If you are down in a game, avoid showing your disappointment, anger or frustration. Do not let your opponent ever suspect that there is anything wrong. A display of emotions will immediately tell him that things are not going well for you. This will only give your opponent greater confidence and motivation and will put you under greater pressure, which you can ill afford. If you are defeated in a match, learn from your mistakes and also from your oppo- nent's. Analyse carefully, by self-examination, the way you played and the tactics that you used against that particular opponent. Examine also your oppon- ent's play and his tactics. It is difficult to store all this knowledge in your head. Many players keep a note book to note down all the strengths and weaknesses of their opponents and how to play them – this is a useful exercise. If you have noted down how you played your opponent the last time it will be so much easier for you the next time.

Respect your opponent and do not think of him as a fool; he will want to win as much as you do. This way you will find it hard to be over-confident during a game, but by the same token, do not hold your oppon- ent in too high esteem. Remember that your opponent may have prepared just as well as you. If this is the case then he will know your strengths and weaknesses. Be prepared for this from the outset of the game.

Conclusion
The Chinese are important figures in the world of table tennis and one of their sayings is, 'We learn from each other'. This is what you need to do – learn from other players about their styles and techniques of playing, their strong points and weak ones. If you learn about someone's table tennis problem, see that it does not become yours. Be an individual with your own style of play and do not copy the top players – remember that Desmond Douglas is Desmond Douglas and if you try to emulate his style you will never be as good as Desmond; you may be better if you are yourself.

Index